THE FOOD AND COOKING OF
TUSCANY

THE FOOD AND COOKING OF TUSCANY

65 CLASSIC DISHES FROM TUSCANY, UMBRIA AND LE MARCHE

VALENTINA HARRIS

PHOTOGRAPHY BY MARTIN BRIGDALE

This edition is published by Aquamarine, an imprint of Anness Publishing Ltd, Hermes House, 88–89 Blackfriars Road, London SE1 8HA; tel. 020 7401 2077; fax 020 7633 9499

www.aquamarinebooks.com; www.annesspublishing.com

If you like the images in this book and would like to investigate using them for publishing, promotions or advertising, please visit our website www.practicalpictures.com for more information.

UK agent: The Manning Partnership Ltd; tel. 01225 478444; fax 01225 478440; sales@manning-partnership.co.uk

UK distributor: Book Trade Services; tel. 0116 2759086; fax 0116 2759090; uksales@booktradeservices.com; exportsales@booktradeservices.com

North American agent/distributor: National Book Network; tel. 301 459 3366; fax 301 429 5746; www.nbnbooks.com

Australian agent/distributor: Pan Macmillan Australia; tel. 1300 135 113; fax 1300 135 103; customer.service@macmillan.com.au

New Zealand agent/distributor: David Bateman Ltd; tel. (09) 415 7664; fax (09) 415 8892

Publisher: Joanna Lorenz
Senior Editor: Lucy Doncaster
Project Editor: Kate Eddison
Copy Editors: Catherine Best and Jan Cutler
Designer: Simon Daley
Photographer: Martin Brigdale
Food Stylist: Valentina Harris
Prop Stylist: Helen Trent
Illustrator: David Cook
Indexer: Diana LeCore
Proofreading Manager: Lindsay Zamponi
Editorial Reader: Lauren Farnsworth
Production Controller: Mai-Ling Collyer

NOTES
Bracketed terms are intended for American readers. For all recipes, quantities are given in both metric and imperial measures and, where appropriate, in standard cups and spoons. Follow one set of measures, but not a mixture, because they are not interchangeable.

- Standard spoon and cup measures are level. 1 tsp = 5ml, 1 tbsp = 15ml, 1 cup = 250ml/8fl oz. Australian standard tablespoons are 20ml. Australian readers should use 3 tsp in place of 1 tbsp for measuring small quantities.
- American pints are 16fl oz/2 cups. American readers should use 20fl oz/2.5 cups in place of 1 pint when measuring liquids.
- Electric oven temperatures in this book are for conventional ovens. When using a fan oven, the temperature will probably need to be reduced by about 10–20°C/20–40°F. Since ovens vary, you should check with your manufacturer's instruction book for guidance.
- The nutritional analysis given for each recipe is calculated per portion (i.e. serving or item), unless otherwise stated. If the recipe gives a range, such as Serves 4–6, then the nutritional analysis will be for the smaller portion size, i.e. 6 servings.
- Measurements for sodium do not include salt added to taste.
- Medium (US large) eggs are used unless otherwise stated.

Front cover shows Stewed Beans – for recipe, see page 98.

A CIP catalogue record for this book is available from the British Library.

ETHICAL TRADING POLICY
At Anness Publishing we believe that business should be conducted in an ethical and ecologically sustainable way, with respect for the environment and a proper regard to the replacement of the natural resources we employ.

As a publisher, we use a lot of wood pulp to make high-quality paper for printing, and that wood commonly comes from spruce trees. We are therefore currently growing more than 750,000 trees in three Scottish forest plantations: Berrymoss (130 hectares/320 acres), West Touxhill (125 hectares/ 305 acres) and Deveron Forest (75 hectares/ 185 acres). The forests we manage contain more than 3.5 times the number of trees employed each year in making paper for the books we manufacture.

Because of this ongoing ecological investment programme, you, as our customer, can have the pleasure and reassurance of knowing that a tree is being cultivated on your behalf to naturally replace the materials used to make the book you are holding.

Our forestry programme is run in accordance with the UK Woodland Assurance Scheme (UKWAS) and will be certified by the internationally recognized Forest Stewardship Council (FSC). The FSC is a non-government organization dedicated to promoting responsible management of the world's forests. Certification ensures forests are managed in an environmentally sustainable and socially responsible way. For further information about this scheme, go to www.annesspublishing.com/trees

CONTENTS

A DIVERSE LANDSCAPE

Breathtakingly stunning coastlines, verdant green plains awash with vineyards, precipitous snow-clad mountains, rolling hills topped by ancient towns, and swathes of olive groves – Tuscany, Umbria and Le Marche are unparalleled in their charm. Three of the four regions that make up the beautiful territory of Central Italy (the fourth region, Lazio, lies further south), these regions are geographically close, nestling together around the splendid Apennine mountain range. They share a glorious landscape dotted with hill-top medieval towns, but there are subtle differences in landscape, climate and agriculture, which makes their respective cuisines quite distinctive. Despite these differences, their traditional dishes all share a rustic simplicity and demonstrate a sincere, unassuming joy of food.

TUSCANY – A GREEN AND GENTLE LANDSCAPE

One of the largest regions of Italy, Tuscany is blessed with exceptional beauty and has long been one of Italy's most loved regions. It stretches along the north-western coast of Italy, bound inland by mountains to the north and east. Much of Tuscany's landscape is green and fertile – ideal for agriculture. The two most renowned crops of Tuscany – olives and grapes – flourish on these warm, gentle hills.

The Arno is the region's major river, flowing down from the Apennines to provide plentiful irrigation for crops in the fields from Florence to the coast. The cities of Florence and Pisa are both built on this majestic waterway. Just off the coast lies a little cluster of coastal islands, including the island of Elba (site of Napoleon's first period of exile), where the delicious dessert wine Aleatico is produced.

Generally, the climate in Tuscany is mild all year round. A cold snap is rare, though much feared as it can cause untold damage to the region's precious olive trees and vineyards. In spring and autumn Tuscany remains mostly dry and sunny, but there is sufficient rain to give the crops a good soaking. Winter brings pleasantly mild days near the coast, though it can get very cold at night. The temperature high in the mountains often falls below freezing, with enough snowfall for skiing to be enjoyed at resorts such as Abetone, north of Florence.

UMBRIA – FERTILE HILLSIDES

The region of Umbria, though less well-known than that of Tuscany, is no less beautiful. The towns that dot the hillsides are steeped in history. Umbria falls very roughly into two distinct landscapes. To the east, the Apennine mountains march proudly down from the north; in the lower-lying west, the mountains give way to gentle rolling hills that are much more conducive to farming. Agriculture remains the chief occupation of the area. The olive oil produced here is sweet, and considered by many to be the finest in Italy; the vineyards make delightful wines; and the wheat crop is made into the best-quality pasta.

BELOW *Tuscany, Umbria and Le Marche stretch across the centre of Italy.*

BELOW RIGHT *The familiar 'boot' shape of Italy is surrounded by seas, which provide plentiful supplies of fish and shellfish to the coastal towns.*

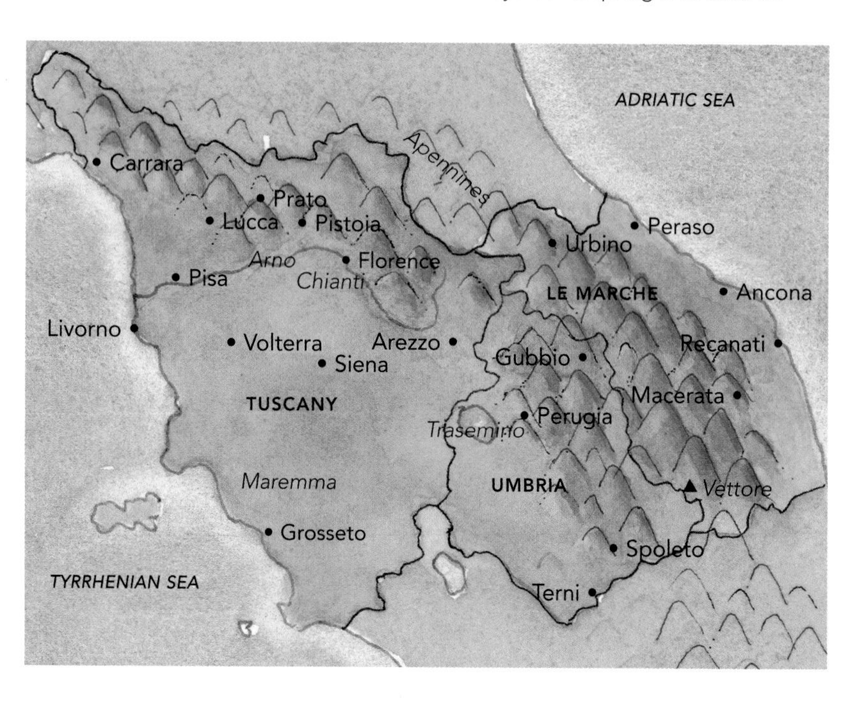

The highest mountain in the Umbrian Apennines is Monte Vettore. Snow-capped for much of the year, it dominates the intriguing landscape of the Piano Grande, a flat area ringed by high mountains. This dried-up lake bed still floods, creating large shallow ponds, with vegetation submerged under a layer of water. Some of the ground is cultivated, though much of it is effectively a huge natural hay meadow, with flocks of sheep roaming the slopes, tended by shepherds with their dogs. In April the snow retreats and the flat grassland glows with pale purple crocuses, some of which are harvested to produce saffron.

The Umbrian climate runs to extremes, as it has no sea breezes to cool and refresh the atmosphere. There is roasting heat in summer, deep snow in winter, and violent storms can occur at any time.

LE MARCHE – UNDISCOVERED MOUNTAINS

The peaceful region of Le Marche, on the eastern coast of Central Italy, has seen an influx of foreign tourists in the last decade, thanks to its beautiful coastlines and idyllic countryside; one of the things that makes this region so attractive is its breathtakingly unspoilt vista.

The landscape is characterized by a rugged and mountainous hinterland that gently rolls toward the Adriatic Sea to the east, and this unforgiving terrain forces most of the population to live near the coast. The sparsely populated inland areas are home to remote mountain gorges, waterfalls and caves. The Adriatic coast has many beach resorts and fishing towns, such as Recanati, where people flock to enjoy delicious fish and shellfish dishes at the local seafront restaurants.

Snow falls as early as autumn on the peaks of the Sibillini Mountains, to the south of the region, and remains on the mountain tops until the end of May. Spring weather is quite unpredictable, though tender plants such as tomatoes and sweet peppers are planted out in early May. Summers are hot and dry, and there is usually very little rain until late September. Autumn in Le Marche is beautiful and full of colour, with the woods and forests vibrant with yellow, orange, red and russet brown leaves. There are many wild mushrooms to be found in the forests, as well as the elusive and rare white truffles, which are sought by eager truffle hunters during the autumnal months.

ABOVE LEFT *The splendid grandeur of the Piano Grande on the border of Umbria and Le Marche is enhanced by a wonderful display of wildflowers.*

ABOVE *Vines flourish on the hills of the picturesque Chianti region in Tuscany.*

BELOW *Medieval houses dot the idyllic hillsides around the small town of San Gimignano.*

AN ANCIENT HISTORY

The central area of Italy has its own distinct character, which sets it apart from the hot, passionate south and the cool, cosmopolitan north. Treasured traditions are alive and well within the age-old walls of the rural medieval villages and world-famous Renaissance towns. The superb cuisines of Tuscany, Umbria and Le Marche are based on a cornucopia of local ingredients, which are meticulously and lovingly prepared according to cooking methods handed down over generations, some even dating back to pre-Roman times.

TUSCAN WEALTH

The original inhabitants of Tuscany, along with Umbria and other parts of Italy, were the Etruscans, about whom little is known. They inhabited the area from around 700BC to 100BC, when they succumbed to the Romans, who established many towns. Archaeological evidence shows it may have been the Etruscans who first enjoyed cooking and eating pasta.

The Middle Ages saw the cities of Pisa, Siena, Arezzo, Pistoia, Lucca, and especially Florence become wealthy thanks to textile manufacture, trade, banking and agriculture. By the 12th century, Florence was beginning to overshadow all its neighbouring cities. It was ruled by an oligarchy of wealthy aristocrats, most importantly the Medici family who became dominant in the 15th century. Under the patronage of these wealthy families, arts and literature flourished as nowhere else in Europe.

The skill of cooking and presenting elaborate dishes was first recognized as a real art form at around this time. Great care and attention was given to the preparation of dishes in the kitchens of the aristocracy to impress both friends and rivals, and thus Tuscan cuisine developed and prospered alongside sculpture, painting and music. There was also a wealth of new ingredients available for the first time, thanks to the Medici family's connections with rulers from countries far and wide.

Such was the quality of Tuscan cooking that some even claim that France owes its legendary culinary skill to Italy, and Florence in particular, through the marriage of Catherine de' Medici to Henry, second son of King Francis I of France, in 1533. Upon her marriage, Catherine was followed to France by her kitchen staff, armed with her favourite recipes, and the cooks of Florence taught the cooks of France to prepare dishes fit for a royal court.

BELOW *The wedding banquet of Grand Duke Ferdinand I of Tuscany, a wealthy Medici ruler, who controlled Florence from 1587 to 1609, would have showcased a whole host of elaborate dishes using exotic ingredients.*

BELOW RIGHT *The imposing duomo dominates the skyline of Florence to this day.*

LEFT *A truffle hunter and his dog search for truffles in the Umbrian forests.*

ABOVE *The Ducal Palace nestles within the walled city of Urbino, demonstrating the stunning Renaissance architecture of Le Marche.*

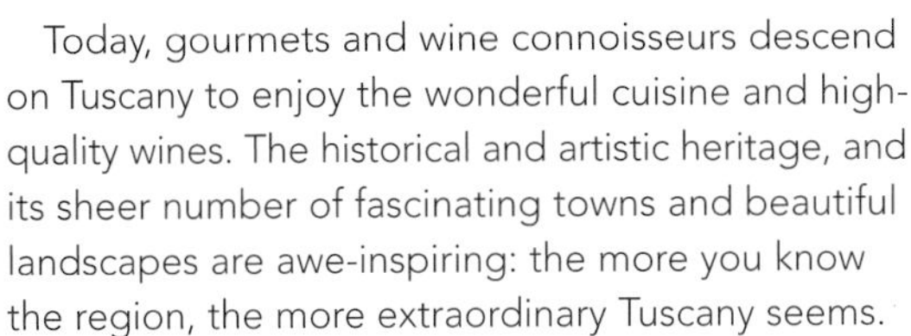

Today, gourmets and wine connoisseurs descend on Tuscany to enjoy the wonderful cuisine and high-quality wines. The historical and artistic heritage, and its sheer number of fascinating towns and beautiful landscapes are awe-inspiring: the more you know the region, the more extraordinary Tuscany seems.

UMBRIAN SPIRITUALITY

This landlocked region of Central Italy is named after the Umbri tribe, who settled in the region during the 6th century BC. Invasions by the Etruscans and then the Romans followed. Nearly a millennium later, like other areas of Italy, Umbria suffered hardship with the fall of the Roman Empire. The struggle between Barbarians and Byzantines created a power vacuum that began to be filled by Christianity, and by the 4th century Christian bishops became the cultural and spiritual figureheads of the region. This is the home of St Francis of Assisi, Saint Scholastica and many other holy men and women. The area became a centre of learning, due to the number of Franciscan and Benedictine monasteries, and the respected University of Perugia was established in 1308.

Umbria is affectionately known as the green heart of Italy. Its cuisine has not generally been influenced by neighbouring regions or nations, and remains based around local ingredients, such as game, fresh and cured pork, lentils and spelt flour, freshwater fish from Lake Trasimeno, and of course precious truffles.

LE MARCHE TRADITION

Although Le Marche borders Umbria, and is within easy reach of Tuscany and the capital city of Rome, it maintains a very strong sense of its own identity. People have lived on this fertile landscape since at least 6000BC, thousands of years before the Etruscans. Via the port of Ancona, they established links with the Ancient Greeks, and later the Gauls. Two and a half millennia later, a Gallic influence is still apparent in the dialects spoken in the north.

Ancona became the gateway through which Christianity entered Italy, paving the way for battles for control of the region during the Renaissance. This era saw huge fluctuations in power between the ruling families.

Historically, the region of Le Marche formed a natural boundary between the Papal and Imperial lands. Napoleon temporarily interrupted the Papal rule of Le Marche but it was resumed until the battle of Castelfiardo in 1860, when the Piedmontese army of the House of Savoy defeated the Papal army. Le Marche was thereafter absorbed into the new nation of Italy, in November 1861.

Le Marche history lives and breathes in the rich tapestry of art and architecture of the walled cities, in the taste of the centuries-old classic cuisine and excellent wines, and in the many ancient pagan and religious festivals that are still celebrated today. Changing times have left their mark on the region, but all the important traditions remain.

A TIMELESS CUISINE

Throughout Italy, there is a great sense of respect for all the different elements that make a region's cuisine unique, and a delight in promoting local dishes and ingredients. The varied histories and landscapes of Tuscany, Umbria and Le Marche have created distinctive regional cuisines that are celebrated around the world. Recipes that derive from medieval kitchens or Renaissance banquets have survived the passage of time and are still found today, perhaps with minor adaptations, in the restaurants and homes of Central Italy.

HISTORICAL FOODS

Although the three regions of Tuscany, Umbria and Le Marche have their own very individual recipes, ingredients, culinary traditions and habits, they do share one common factor: all have a set of recipes that were historically created for the wealthy, and another set eaten by the poor. Only the nobility or the clergy would have been able to afford expensive ingredients such as salt, sugar, fine flour or spices from faraway lands, exotic fruit and vegetables, the best cuts of meat, and the most valuable fish or shellfish. The poorer people, mainly peasant farmers or simple craftsmen, would have lived off a completely different fare, eating a basic and more repetitive diet. Both types of recipes survive today.

The temperate climate and fertile landscape mean that a diverse range of foods are produced in the region. In Central Italy, summers are hotter and longer than in the north. Consequently, soft fruit and vegetables such as tomatoes flourish, and there are plenty of tomato-based dishes to be found. However, unlike the south, the winters can be extremely cold, especially inland, making it also possible to grow green leafy vegetables that require a sharp frost to develop the best flavour. These vegetables, along with carbohydrates such as pasta, bread, grains and pulses, are used to make hearty, rib-sticking soups and stews that pepper the traditional menu amid the more familiar pasta dishes, risottos, salads and antipasti.

BELOW *There is evidence to suggest that pasta has been cooked in Italian kitchens for thousands of years, and this tradition remains today.*

ABOVE LEFT *Olives are harvested throughout Tuscany for their precious oil.*

ABOVE *Chestnuts, which are used to make flour for bread, pasta and cakes, litter the forest floor in the hills of Tuscany.*

THE CUISINE OF TUSCANY

It is the more basic peasant dishes that have defined the traditional cuisine of Tuscany most clearly. Fragrant local olive oil, for example, has always been chosen as the main cooking fat instead of the more expensive options of butter or pork fat. Along the coast, full use has always been made of the daily fish and shellfish catch, with the port city of Livorno leading the way with its fantastic fish soup, cacciucco. What is still evident throughout Tuscany is the historical continuity and respect for the classic dishes, with each individual area maintaining its own unique specialities and local culinary traditions.

Bread – the basic ingredient Next to olive oil, bread is the most fundamental part of Tuscan cuisine. Different breads are made all over the region and come in a multitude of forms and flavours: long, flattish loaves, unsalted bread, crown-shaped loaves, bitesized crostini, schiacciata all'olio (a type of focaccia), fragrant rosemary rolls, not to mention a fabulous variety of sweet breads, such as buccellato from Lucca, or the Florentine schiacciata all'uva, which is prepared only during the grape harvest.

The absence of salt in Tuscany's traditional bread is a reminder of a time when, for many, salt would have been simply too expensive to add to the dough. Many of the region's most characteristic recipes are created with bread as the main ingredient.

More unusual bread is made from chestnut flour. In the Tuscan mountains, chestnuts are harvested, dried and then milled into flour for making bread, as well as pasta, griddle cakes known as necci, and the delicious cake called castagnaccio.

FAMOUS TUSCAN BREAD DISHES

- La panzanella, made with hard bread which is soaked in water, squeezed dry, and then mixed with fresh vegetables and dressed with oil and vinegar.
- Pappa al pomodoro, a deliciously thick soup made with bread, tomatoes and basil.
- Ribollita, meaning 'boiled again', a reheated vegetable and pulse soup, to which bread is added the second time round to make the soup stretch a bit further.

ABOVE *Two fishermen unload their eel and freshwater fish catch from Lake Trasimeno, Umbria.*

ABOVE RIGHT *Farmers in Tuscany harvest grapes, ready to make the world-famous wines.*

Local specialities from Tuscany Many of the region's towns are known for specific dishes. Florence, for example, has the huge Fiorentina steak; nearby Prato is where the much-loved dunking biscuits, cantucci, were created; Pisa is dominated by the truffles of nearby San Miniato, as well as locally caught eels and a dried salted cod, or stoccafisso.

In the Maremma, a flat marshy land, the most celebrated local dish is named acquacotta, 'cooked water'. This very basic peasant dish would originally have been made with nothing more than bread, water and a little olive oil, with a sprinkling of the sharp local Pecorino cheese, although nowadays a number of other ingredients are added as toppings.

THE CUISINE OF UMBRIA

Umbrian cooking is hearty and filling. Anchovies, olives, artichokes and capers are primary ingredients, along with pork, pigeon and wild game.

Umbrian cooks use ancient spit-roasting techniques to cook game. A local wood pigeon or other game bird is turned slowly on the spit while being brushed with la ghiotta, a traditional game marinade made of red wine, olive oil, pancetta, capers, vinegar, olives, anchovies, onion, garlic, juniper berries or cloves, sage leaves and lemon juice – a recipe that has remained unchanged for hundreds of years.

Delicacies from the forests The most prized ingredient of this region is the black truffle, tartufo nero. Black truffles ripen during the winter and are sniffed out from underground by specially trained dogs. The truffles are a highly valued find in the rich, black soil, their whereabouts a closely held secret passed from generation to generation. With their pungent, distinctly earthy taste and musty aroma, truffles are unmatched in flavour when shaved over freshly made thin ribbons of pasta, or sprinkled over an egg fried in butter, or added to savoury sauces.

In springtime, locals roam through fields and woods foraging for the elusive stalks of the local wild asparagus, asparagi selvatici. The stalks are pencil-thin, delicate and tender, and make a delicious accompaniment to game and pork.

Local specialities from Umbria Perugian cuisine is perhaps the most typical of the whole region. The olive oil produced here is of tremendously high quality. Norcia is noted for its butchered and cured pork meat, and the production of world-class salumeria (cold meats). There is even a word used to define this special skill: Norcineria.

The people of Terni, further south, enjoy a diet rich in meat, especially game. The area is also famous for its unsalted bread. Baked in a wood-fired oven, this delicious, crusty bread is perfect with the local cured pork meats, or sliced and toasted on a grill set over glowing wood embers, rubbed with garlic, drizzled with olive oil and served with stews or topped with truffle slices.

Freshwater fish dishes are popular in this inland region. The fish is roasted over an open wood flame to char it on the outside. It is then skinned and cleaned, filleted and dressed with plenty of extra virgin olive oil, a little salt, pepper and garlic.

THE CUISINE OF LE MARCHE

The food and cooking of Le Marche makes the most of the bounty of the sea as well as produce from the land. The port of Ancona has traded in exotic ingredients from countries to the east for centuries. There is always something joyous about the preparation and consumption of food in this region, a sense of tremendous happiness and pleasure derived from making and eating the traditional dishes. The huge number of small farms testify to the area's rich agricultural heritage.

Meat and fish recipes The local cuisine is dominated by the strong flavours of many meat recipes – principally the rich roasted pork dish known as porchetta. Favourite meats in this region also include veal, rabbit, game birds such as guinea fowl, pigeon and quail, as well as chicken and goose. Both meat and fish are usually cooked with fennel, garlic and rosemary, or in the potacchio style, with onion, tomato, rosemary and white wine. Also worth a very special mention is the delicious naturally-aged cured ham, prosciutto di Carpegna, which, like Parma ham, is traditionally cured in a small area blessed by a microclimate that ensures uniquely tasty results.

ABOVE *A wonderful selection of mushrooms is displayed at a festival in Le Marche.*

The local fish soup, actually more of a stew, is called brodetto. This is the most famous fish dish of the Adriatic coast and recipes vary from one coastal town to another. Brodetto traditionally includes red and grey mullet, cuttlefish or squid, oil, garlic and saffron, and is usually served on fried or toasted bread. There are many other popular recipes using locally caught sole, bream, clams and mussels from the port of Ancona, as well as stoccafisso (dried cod), but brodetto remains the most symbolic and defining fish dish of Le Marche.

Local specialities from Le Marche A typical speciality is the large juicy olives, which are stuffed with meat, rolled in flour, egg and breadcrumbs, and deep-fried. The Romans and Carthaginians are thought to have enjoyed these unique extra-large green olives centuries ago.

Pecorino, especially the softer, young Pecorino, made from local ewe's milk, is the favourite cheese. Desserts in this region are not usually overwhelmingly sweet and are often based on pale, soft cheeses such as ricotta.

LEFT *Black truffles, one of the most valuable delicacies in Italy, are sniffed out by trained dogs in Umbria's forests.*

FESTIVALS AND CELEBRATIONS

Italians love an excuse for a party. As well as an array of religious celebrations, there is a vast number of small local festivals that take place all over the country, especially during the summer. These celebrate anything and everything: the mushroom crop, pasta dishes, the local saint's day or a political affiliation. Anyone is welcome to join in the festivities, which usually include food, wine and music, and a wonderful sense of fun. Small local celebrations such as these are often advertised at the roadside, via a hand-painted sign, and are really worth a detour.

RIGHT *Beautifully presented bomboniera are distributed to each guest at the end of an Italian wedding.*

CHRISTMAS

All over Italy, the solemn rituals of Christmas Eve (in Italian, Vigilia – meaning 'keeping watch') are celebrated. The traditional Vigilia feast involves fish, and is made up of seven dishes to represent the seven sacraments, with simple pasta dishes that do not contain any meat, at least until after the celebration of the midnight Mass. Some people like to eat a light meal before the Mass, followed by a huge celebratory feast afterwards, featuring fresh pasta, roasted meat, guinea fowl, and traditional cakes and pastries. After all this feasting, Christmas Day and St Stephen's Day (Boxing Day) tend to be much quieter days, largely devoted to visiting family and friends.

EPIPHANY

Traditionally, Epiphany is the day when gifts are exchanged. La Befana, the warty old witch, comes to visit on her broomstick, bringing presents for the good children and a lump of coal for those who have been naughty. Special cakes are prepared in honour of this day, sometimes baked in the embers of the fire for Befana to find when she comes down the chimney.

BELOW *The great Tuscan tradition of the Befana parade, taking place on the streets of Florence during Epiphany.*

CARNIVAL

The most important day of Carnival is Martedi Grasso, the last day before Ash Wednesday, which marks the beginning of Lent and the long quiet period of self-denial. Martedi Grasso (Fat Tuesday) is a wild day of feasting before Lent, a final thrilling moment of pure indulgence. In Tuscany, traditional parades bring plenty of noisy fun. During Carnival, the custom is to fry great batches of sweet sfrappé, simple sugared pastry strips flavoured with a little wine.

EASTER

In the past, meat was never eaten on Good Friday. Although this is no longer an official Church rule, it is still respected by some religious households. So fish and vegetables, usually simply cooked, are served on this day, which for many is a time of quiet reflection.

In some Italian homes a variety of flat omelettes, called frittatas, along with an assortment of sausages and other meats, are served on Holy Saturday with pane di Pasqua or Easter bread. Easter Sunday is celebrated with special breads and pastries, as well as the main Easter feast, with the agnello Pasquale (Easter lamb) as the centrepiece of the meal.

One of the most joyous of Italian traditions, Easter Monday (Pasquetta) is the unofficial start of spring and a chance to get reacquainted with family, friends, and the great outdoors. Italian Catholics know it as the day to remember the

women of the sepulchre, including Mary Magdalene. However, for most Italians, Pasquetta is a secular holiday, and a day of picnics. Families and friends go out in droves to the mountains or the beaches and set up camp with packed lunches or portable barbecues. They eat frittatas (omelettes) or hard-boiled eggs and an assortment of grilled meats. 'Natale con i tuoi, Pasqua con chi vuoi', goes the Italian saying, which translates as, 'Christmas with your family, Easter with the friends of your choice'.

FRITELLE FESTIVAL

This festival takes place in the beautiful walled village of Montefioralle on the Sunday following St Joseph's Day in March. Fritelle, fried rice cakes, are made in a big cauldron of oil and everyone shares in the eating.

TARTUFO FESTIVAL

This is the black truffle festival, which takes place in the medieval Umbrian town of Norcia on the last weekend of February. Although not as highly prized as white truffles, the black truffles from this region are some of the finest in Italy.

PORCINO MUSHROOM FESTIVAL

The most famous Italian mushroom is celebrated in the town of Ronta in Tuscany at the end of the summer, where an entire menu based on porcini mushrooms is cooked and eaten.

THE PALIO

This famous horse race occurs twice a year in Siena, Tuscany, on the 2nd July and 16th August. Ten horseriders compete in the race, representing the contrades, or districts, of Siena. Festivities begin 3 days prior to the horse race, however, with banquets and parades for each contrade competing.

BAPTISMS

This is a very important occasion for all Catholic Italians. The church ceremony is solemn, but it is followed by a joyful gathering of family and friends and an enormous feast where the baby, parents and godparents are the special guests.

WEDDINGS

Individual traditions attached to weddings vary tremendously from one place to another in Italy, but the occasion is always as grand as possible and no expense is spared. Wedding feasts often involve many hours of celebratory dining at the table with a long succession of antipasti, pasta, meat and fish courses, desserts, and finally the wedding cake. All of this is washed down with copious quantities of wine and many opportunities to raise a glass to the happy couple with a brindisi (toast). Guests always expect to go home with a bomboniera, a little package of sugared almonds with a small present attached – there is usually one for each person.

ABOVE LEFT *As well as religious celebrations, Italy's villages host a variety of unusual festivals, such as this chestnut festival in Le Marche.*

ABOVE *The porcino mushroom is celebrated by a street festival in the small Tuscan town of Ronta, where a wide range of mushroom-based dishes are served.*

CLASSIC INGREDIENTS

The key to all Italian cooking is high-quality basic ingredients. Most Italian dishes are actually very simple and focus on just a few fundamental elements – this could be a piece of meat bought from a local butcher, a tender home-grown vegetable picked from the garden, or some delicate fresh pasta made that morning at the kitchen table – so it is vital that these should be as fresh as can be, sourced locally if possible and, most importantly, in season. From freshwater fish, cured meats and tasty cheeses to seasonal fruits, regional vegetables and substantial beans, the finest ingredients are crucial to good taste.

FISH AND SHELLFISH

The coastal areas of Tuscany and Le Marche have a good supply of all kinds of fish and shellfish from the Mediterranean sea, but freshwater fish also appears on the regions' menus, especially in landlocked Umbria, where recipes for pike and eel dishes are traditional favourites around Easter time. Usually, however, Italian cooks take whatever the fishermen have to offer that particular day, choosing a recipe based on what is available: for example, one of the best mixed fish dishes is the renowned Tuscan fish stew, cacciucco, which is made of at least five different varieties of seafood.

The Italian tradition of eating salted cod (baccalà) or air-dried cod (stoccafisso) persists from the time when cod had to be preserved in this way on its long journey to Italy from the North Sea fishing grounds. The dry, salty fish pieces are soaked well before being used in recipes, including tasty fritters, for which the fish is coated in batter and fried.

POULTRY AND GAME

Chickens have been reared on local farms in Central Italy for centuries. One of Tuscany's best-loved recipes is pollo al mattone (brick chicken), which is thought to date back as far as Etruscan times. In this recipe, the chicken is grilled (broiled) between two hot bricks over the embers of a fire.

Wild boar are hunted in Tuscany and Umbria every autumn and are then used to make a traditional rich stew with tomatoes and red wine, known as cinghiale alla cacciatora. Wild boar meat also goes into creating strong, flavourful sausages, which provide hearty winter fare for the colder months.

Umbrian cooks excel in concocting rich game bird dishes, such as quaglia alla maniera di Todi, a speciality quail dish (also made with wood pigeon) from the pretty town of Todi. Rabbit and guinea fowl are also popular game meats, and at Christmas time, most Central Italians prefer to eat locally reared capons or guinea fowl, rather than a turkey.

BELOW *From left to right, fresh red mullet, a selection of mixed fish and shellfish for cacciucco, succulent sausages, and Parmesan.*

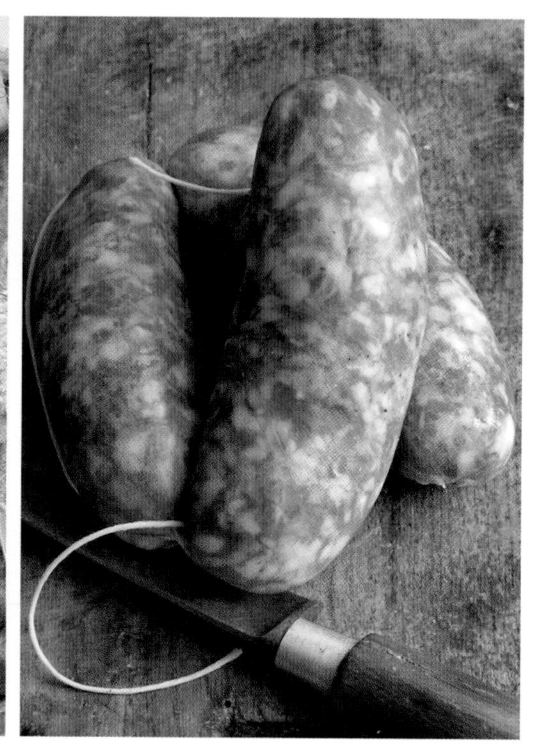

MEAT

The recipes of Tuscany and Umbria feature a great deal of meat, both fresh and cured. Perhaps the most typical and well-known meat recipe of Tuscany is the huge, tender steak known simply as la fiorentina. This mouth-watering piece of meat is served simply grilled (broiled) with a little oil, rosemary, salt, and sometimes garlic. Umbria is particularly renowned for its cured pork products, especially salami and prosciutto. Until quite recently, the traditional diet in Le Marche contained very little meat, though dishes were often given extra flavour with some precious pork fat or pancetta.

In inland rural areas, the coming of winter means the slaughter of the family pig, which provides cured meat, sausages and pork fat to last throughout the cold winter weather. Lardo di Colonnata (cured pork fat) is a famous Tuscan speciality, which is served sliced so thinly that it is almost transparent, and then laid over a warm slice of toasted polenta or bread.

DAIRY PRODUCE

The people of Central Italy love a sharp and tasty sheep's cheese, such as Pecorino, and many kinds are produced throughout the region. Grated Parmesan cheese is sprinkled over pasta and other dishes, as elsewhere in Italy, and bland, soft ricotta is ideal for a tasty dessert or mixed into a savoury pasta filling. Butter and milk are the principal ingredients in béchamel or white sauce, of which the origin is disputed, but Italians claim it was invented by Medici cooks who then took it to France in the 16th century.

WHITE SAUCE

MAKES ABOUT 600ML/1 PINT/2½ CUPS

75g/3oz/6 tbsp unsalted butter
60ml/4 tbsp plain (all-purpose) flour
600ml/1 pint/2½ cups milk
pinch of sea salt
pinch of freshly grated nutmeg

1 Melt the butter in a pan, then stir in the flour over a low heat using a wooden spoon until a paste (roux) is formed.

2 Pour in all the milk, stirring or whisking constantly to prevent lumps forming.

3 Add the salt and nutmeg to taste, then simmer gently for about 15 minutes, stirring constantly.

4 When the sauce is thick enough to coat the back of the spoon, remove from the heat.

5 Cover the surface with a little cold water to prevent a skin forming. Set aside until required.

ABOVE *From left to right, blanched almonds and pine nuts, juicy red grapes, exquisite black truffles, and seasonal asparagus.*

FRUIT AND NUTS

Citrus fruits appear on the market stalls all over Italy in the winter. Oranges and tangerines tend to be eaten fresh while lemons are an important ingredient for many dishes, both sweet and savoury. Lemon juice is a popular dressing for vegetables in Central Italy: it is drizzled along with good-quality olive oil over freshly steamed greens or other vegetables.

The favourite fruits of the summer months include cherries, peaches, apricots, nectarines and plums, eaten fresh or used in cakes, tarts, ice cream or sticky syrup. Strawberries, the first of the soft fruits, are traditionally served with a dressing of lemon or orange juice or white wine and a good sprinkling of sugar. Towards the end of the season, wild woodland strawberries (fragoline di bosco) are gathered in warmer rural areas. In July and August, melon is served with prosciutto, the two flavours and textures working perfectly together, while juicy pink watermelon is eaten simply as a thirst-quenching snack. Grapes are not only made into wine, but also eaten fresh or used as a special topping for harvest bread (schiacciata d'uva) or a juicy accompaniment to the rich, meaty sausages of the region.

The end of the summer is marked by the arrival of the golden-orange persimmon, with its fine skin and delicate flesh. The sweet chestnut season starts in late October, and in Tuscany, chestnut flour is used to make a moist cake called castagnaccio. In some areas, a little chestnut flour is still added to bread dough to give it a special local flavour. Almonds are used in a whole host of traditional desserts and cakes.

VEGETABLES

Fresh vegetables are an essential part of the cook's resources in Central Italy, and their seasonality and taste are valued far above their appearance. The most typical vegetables of the region feature across the menu, in appetizers, soups, stews, and as side dishes; no meal is complete without them.

Cavolo nero (black cabbage) is harvested in Tuscany during the winter and early spring. It has a strong taste, and is eaten braised, or as a nourishing ingredient in hearty soups such as the classic ribollita. Onions (red, brown and white) and garlic are fundamental ingredients for almost all savoury dishes in Central Italy. Garlic is widely used in its dried form throughout the summer, autumn and winter, but in the spring it is harvested when still soft and slightly green, which means it has a milder taste and breaks down more quickly during the cooking process.

Spring brings the new artichokes, beginning with the smaller varieties, which have a unique, strong flavour that blends well with pasta. Fresh beans and peas also mark the start of the spring season. The early broad (fava) beans are often eaten raw, with a slice or two of salty Pecorino cheese, while deliciously sweet fresh peas are stewed with onion and pancetta or prosciutto. The thin wild asparagus of Umbria is found in the countryside throughout the spring season and can be made into a fragrant sauce for spaghetti, or served as a simple side dish.

In high summer, a huge variety of different kinds of courgette (zucchini) are grown in the region. They are especially tasty when cut into little batons,

dipped in batter and deep-fried. Even their flowers are cooked, either fried in batter or stuffed with ricotta cheese and baked in a cool oven. Summers in Tuscany, Umbria and Le Marche are hot enough to produce a good crop of sweet tomatoes, which are used in cooking and also eaten fresh in salads. Plenty are left over to be made into a variety of tomato-based sauces or sun-dried for the winter.

A green salad is almost always a part of the meal in every Italian household – it is immensely beneficial to the digestion and helps to cleanse the palate. Green salads can contain all manner of seasonal lettuces, depending on what is available, and often also wild leaves that have been gathered in the countryside, such as sorrel.

Autumn brings with it the celebrated mushroom and truffle season. Mushrooms are gathered fresh from the fields, then either eaten straight away or dried and reconstituted later to add their strong flavour to pasta dishes, stews or soups. Truffles are a favourite but expensive delicacy – tiny shavings are often added to a bland omelette, where their flavour does not have to compete with other tastes and really shines through.

Olives grow everywhere in these regions, freshly picked in autumn to be marinated, or pressed to make the most delicious olive oil. The large, succulent olives of Le Marche are fat and juicy. They can be stuffed with meat and deep-fried to make the unusual antipasto, olive all'Ascolana, named after the town of Ascoli Piceno, which is surrounded by mountains on three sides.

BASIC TOMATO SAUCE

MAKES ABOUT 600ML/1 PINT/2½ CUPS

900g/2lb fresh tomatoes, skinned and quartered, or 2 x 400g/14oz cans tomatoes, drained and quartered
1 small onion, quartered
1 carrot, quartered
1 celery stick, quartered
1 large parsley sprig
10 fresh basil leaves
sea salt
45ml/3 tbsp extra virgin olive oil (optional)

1 Put the tomatoes, onion, carrot, celery, parsley and basil into a pan. Cover and bring to the boil, then simmer for 30 minutes.

2 Remove the lid and continue to simmer for a further 20 minutes, or until most of the liquid has evaporated.

3 Remove from the heat and push the mixture through a food mill or sieve (strainer). Season to taste with salt, and reheat, adding the oil, if using, just before serving, or using in a recipe.

Skinning tomatoes Plunge the tomatoes into boiling water for 30 seconds, then refresh in cold water. Peel away the skins.

BASIC BREAD DOUGH

MAKES ABOUT 450G/1LB OF DOUGH

35g/1¼oz fresh yeast
300ml/½ pint/1¼ cups warm water
pinch of sugar
450g/1lb/4 cups strong white bread flour, plus extra for dusting
5ml/1 tsp sea salt
15ml/3 tsp olive oil, plus extra for greasing

1 Mix the yeast and water together in a small bowl. Add the sugar and 30ml/2 tbsp of the flour. Leave in a warm place for about 30 minutes, or until it becomes frothy.

2 Put the remaining flour on to the work surface. Make a well in the centre of the flour and pour in the yeast mixture. Work the yeast mixture into the flour, then add the salt and the oil and knead for 10 minutes, or until the dough becomes soft and elastic.

3 Transfer the dough to a large floured bowl, cover with lightly oiled clear film (plastic wrap) and leave to rise in a warm place for 2 hours, or until doubled in size.

Cook's tip This basic bread dough can be used in a variety of recipes, but you can also simply cook the bread as it is. Preheat the oven to 220°C/425°F/Gas 7. Oil a large baking sheet and sprinkle with polenta. To make simple Italian bread, knock back (punch down) the risen dough, and then, with well-oiled hands, pull the dough apart into six pieces. Shape it into rolls, rough rounds, or long, narrow shapes or braids, then lay them on the oiled baking sheet. Brush the surface of the bread gently with a little olive oil mixed with water. Bake for 15 minutes, or until light golden and the underneath sounds hollow when tapped. Allow the bread to cool on a wire rack.

PULSES

Tuscans are known throughout the rest of Italy as mangiafagioli (bean eaters), due to their passion for beans. They cook them in soups and stews, both fresh when available and dried. The most famous and highly valued lentils in Italy come from the area around Castelluccio in Umbria and are pale brown, small, flattish, and require no pre-soaking before cooking. Chickpeas are another common feature of the peasant cooking of these regions, adding flavour and bulk to stews and soups.

GRAINS, POLENTA AND PASTA

Bread is a vital ingredient in many dishes of Tuscany, Umbria and Le Marche, as well as an essential part of any meal. In Tuscany, to make a simple soup more substantial and filling, lightly toasted slices of bread are used to line the bowl before the soup is poured over.

The flour used for making polenta is made by grinding a particular variety of maize (either yellow or white). Polenta flour is also used to make cakes or can be added to wheat flour for specific kinds of bread. Spelt is another grain that makes tasty, gluten-free bread, as well as a nutritious stew or soup, mixed with plenty of fresh vegetables.

Pasta triumphs over bread in Le Marche, where great store is set by home-made pasta. The most traditional pasta dish made in this region is called vincisgrassi, which is a layered dish made with chicken livers and mushrooms, rather like lasagne. Typically, Umbrian pasta consists of substantial,

heavy-duty ombrici or ombricelli, which is very thick spaghetti made from the local durum wheat flour and water. Tuscan pasta includes pappardelle, thumb-wide egg pasta ribbons, often served with a hare sauce; unevenly cut rectangles of egg pasta known as maltagliati; and pici, irregular strands of flour-and-water pasta, which is slightly thicker than spaghetti.

HERBS AND SPICES

Rosemary, with its spiky leaves, is the symbolic taste and perfume of Tuscany. Even the humblest of dishes use this wonderfully fragrant herb to enhance their flavour. Other favourites include basil, which is perfect in summer dishes; sage, which is often added to winter dishes; and flat leaf parsley. Wild fennel fronds and celery leaves are added to many of the traditional dishes of Le Marche.

Fennel seeds, nutmeg and cinnamon are the most commonly used spices in both the sweet and savoury dishes of these regions. Fiery red chilli peppers (peperoncini) feature in some meat and fish dishes, and juniper berries can make all the difference to a rich wild boar stew.

OIL AND VINEGAR

All three regions of Central Italy produce fantastic and world-famous olive oil, the most well known being the peppery olive oil of Tuscany. The vinegar of choice in this part of Italy would always be sharp red or white wine vinegar, never the sweet and sticky balsamic vinegar produced in Modena.

SWEET THINGS

Desserts and cakes are very simple in these regions, and are usually reserved for special times of the year, such as religious festivals. With such a wonderful bounty of fruit available all year round, and the ubiquitous gelateria (ice cream parlour) on the street corner in even the smallest of towns, there is surprisingly little need for a wide range of cakes and desserts to be made at home. Generally speaking, Italians do not have a sweet tooth, though Umbria is famous for its rich chocolate and nougat.

Honey is also very important to these regions, especially in Tuscany, where a vast range of varieties is available, and used in desserts and baking.

ALCOHOLIC DRINKS

Tuscany is famous for the delicious wines of the Chianti area, in particular Brunello di Montalcino and Montepulciano. Sagrantino is one of the best-loved red wines of Umbria, and Le Marche has the delightfully fresh Verdicchio dei Castelli di Iesi, as well as the rich red Rosso di Conero. Vinsanto ('holy wine') is the most popular dessert wine of this area of Italy. Sweet and delicious, it is usually served with hard almond biscuits, known as cantucci.

A huge variety of local liqueurs, which are generally very sweet, are made in all three regions of Central Italy, many of them using seasonal fruits. Mistra, from Le Marche, is very similar in taste to ouzo, with the same aniseed flavour. It can be enjoyed both as an aperitif and to aid digestion at the end of a meal, and is also used in some local cakes and desserts.

BELOW *From left to right, traditional Tuscan maltagliati pasta, yellow polenta, wild fennel, and rich red wine.*

SOUPS AND ANTIPASTI
ZUPPE, MINESTRE E ANTIPASTI

Nutritious, sustaining and adaptable, soups are one of the great pleasures of hearty Italian cooking. Dense, thick soups are almost filling enough to constitute a meal in themselves, whereas lighter, thinner-textured soups can replace the pasta course of a meal, or form part of a longer meal with many courses. In Tuscany, Umbria and Le Marche, hearty soups made using pulses are intrinsic to the culinary culture and traditions of the area. Coming either before or instead of the soup, an antipasto, or several different antipasti, made up of cured meats, fish or vegetables, would be the classic way to begin the meal. Traditionally, the antipasto should be a small, light course, as it is served as an appetizer – literally to stimulate the appetite and to help prepare for the following course, the primo.

SALADS, BROTHS AND DEEP-FRIED BITES

Soups, particularly the nourishing broths made with vegetables, pulses or grains, are synonymous with the simple peasant style of food that is typical of Tuscany, Umbria and Le Marche. Often further enriched with the addition of pork or bacon, as well as ever-present olive oil, they can be an entire meal. Soups that are traditional to this area range from hearty and warming fish soups, such as Ancona Fish Soup, to light and refreshing dishes, such as Tuscan Cold Summer Soup. Clear Chicken Soup with Passatelli, a popular dish in Le Marche, is a sumptuous clear soup, thickened with bread and Parmesan and flavoured with lemon zest.

Bread has always been considered to be far too precious to waste, so stale bread is often used to bulk out the local soups and make them stretch that little bit further. A typical example is the famous Tomato and Bread Soup from Tuscany, made with fresh tomatoes and stale bread, which are boiled together and flavoured with onions, basil and, of course, plenty of rich extra virgin olive oil. Bread dough can also be deep-fried into simple but tasty fritters.

In many restaurants in these regions, a selection of antipasti is offered from a buffet table. Once you have ordered your primo, be it a risotto, pasta or gnocchi, you can help yourself to a small selection of different antipasti to nibble while you are waiting. Antipasti, literally meaning 'before the meal', can range from a simple selection of cured meats, served with pickles and bread, to a much more elaborate dish or light salad. The singular word for antipasti is antipasto, and when ordering from a menu it is normal to order only one per person. Antipasti need to be light and not too filling.

TUSCAN COLD SUMMER SOUP
ZUPPA DEI MORI

The origins of this classic, elegant cold soup date back to the Medici court, and it is believed to have been created for banquets honouring guests from North Africa, hence the name Mori, which translates as Moors. Before the invention of the food processor, the vegetables would have been chopped into tiny pieces and then pounded into a rough purée using a large mortar and pestle. Cooling and delicious, this soup is perfect for serving on hot summer days.

1 Place the cucumber, slices of fennel, chopped celery, lettuce, tomatoes, carrots, lemon, garlic, chilli and basil in the bowl of a food processor, and gradually process all ingredients until well mixed; alternatively, use a blender and blend until smooth.

2 Add 250ml/8fl oz/1 cup water and the extra virgin olive oil, then season with salt and black pepper to taste.

3 Ladle into a serving bowl and chill until required. Serve with croûtons, if you like.

SERVES 6

½ cucumber, peeled and cubed
1 fennel bulb, thinly sliced
1 celery heart, chopped
1 lettuce, chopped
4 tomatoes, peeled, seeded and chopped
3 carrots, quartered
1 lemon, peeled and thinly sliced
3 garlic cloves, chopped
1 dried red chilli, finely chopped
1 bunch fresh basil
75ml/2½fl oz/⅓ cup extra virgin olive oil
sea salt and ground black pepper
croûtons, to serve (optional)

COOK'S TIP

To peel tomatoes, place in a bowl, cover with boiling water and leave for 30 seconds. Refresh under cold water and the skins will peel off easily.

PER PORTION Energy 119kcal/494kJ; Protein 1.3g; Carbohydrate 7.2g, of which sugars 6.9g; Fat 9.7g, of which saturates 1.4g; Cholesterol 0mg; Calcium 33mg; Fibre 2.9g; Sodium 23mg.

SERVES 6

1.5 litres/2½ pints/6¼ cups vegetable, chicken or meat stock
1 large onion, chopped
1.2kg/2½lb very ripe tomatoes, coarsely chopped
120ml/4fl oz/½ cup extra virgin olive oil
400g/14oz stale ciabatta, crusts removed, thinly sliced
3 garlic cloves, crushed
a large handful of fresh basil leaves, chopped
sea salt and ground black pepper

TOMATO AND BREAD SOUP
PAPPA AL POMODORO

This is a very thick, almost solid, soup, which makes the best of the glut of overripe tomatoes at the end of a Tuscan summer. These are combined with that ever-present standby ingredient: stale bread. It is marvellous served lukewarm with plenty of basil and extra olive oil to drizzle over it. It became especially famous during the 1960s when a pop song, sung by Rita Pavone, described how wonderful this soup was. It remains a traditional part of the classic Tuscan menu.

1 Heat the stock gently in a large pan. Meanwhile, put the onion, tomatoes and half the oil in a separate pan and fry together over a gentle heat for 10 minutes, or until softened.

2 Push the onion and tomato mixture through a food mill or sieve (strainer) and add it to the hot stock. Stir thoroughly.

3 Add the bread, garlic and most of the basil, and season to taste.

4 Cover and simmer gently for 45 minutes, or until thick and creamy, stirring occasionally. Stir in the remaining oil, adjust the seasoning if necessary, and add the rest of the basil to taste. Serve hot or at room temperature.

COOK'S TIP

Pushing the soup through a food mill (a mouli) or a wide-meshed sieve (strainer) is essential to get the right texture. Do not be tempted to blitz it in a food processor, or it will be too smooth.

PER PORTION Energy 285kcal/1194kJ; Protein 5g; Carbohydrate 28g, of which sugars 7.2g; Fat 17.9g, of which saturates 2.5g; Cholesterol 0mg; Calcium 64mg; Fibre 2.6g; Sodium 243mg.

ANCONA FISH SOUP
BRODETTO ALL'ANCONETANA

Although the diminutive name used locally to describe this dish would make you think you were getting a simple soup, it is actually a chunky and substantial stew. Traditionally, 13 different varieties of fish are used in brodetto, which is symbolic of the great port of Ancona. Among these you would always find scorpion fish, gurnard, eel, sea cricket and red mullet. Because the fish are added whole, bones and all, you need plenty of time to leisurely wade through the process of removing the fish from the bone, then enjoy the fish juices with some crusty bread. There are no other ingredients of any note, so the freshness and variety of the fish is the most important part of the dish.

SERVES 4 TO 6

60ml/4 tbsp extra virgin olive oil
1 onion, chopped
1 garlic clove, chopped
90ml/6 tbsp white or red wine vinegar
300g/11oz canned tomatoes, sieved (strained) or coarsely chopped
900g/2lb mixed whole fish, such as small monkfish, red mullet, whiting or scorpion fish
sea salt and ground black pepper
crusty bread, to serve

1 Put the oil in a very large pan, add the onion and garlic, and fry over medium heat for 5 minutes, or until soft.

2 Gradually add the vinegar, stirring constantly, until the sharp vinegar smell has disappeared.

3 Add the canned tomatoes, stir and simmer for 10 minutes. Gradually add the fish, one at a time, starting with the largest.

4 Cook, stirring gently, for 30 minutes, until the fish is cooked through. Serve with crusty bread.

PER PORTION Energy 389kcal/1627kJ; Protein 27.4g; Carbohydrate 29g, of which sugars 4.8g; Fat 18.9g, of which saturates 2.8g; Cholesterol 68mg; Calcium 46mg; Fibre 2.7g; Sodium 207mg.

CLEAR CHICKEN SOUP WITH PASSATELLI
PASSATELLI IN BRODO

This is one of the oldest and most traditional of all the dishes of Le Marche and it belongs both to this region and to certain parts of Emilia Romagna, although the recipe does vary slightly. The word 'passatelli' comes from the verb 'passare', meaning to pass, which refers to the mixture being forced through the widest holes of the food mill or ricer, thus 'passing' into the soup itself. A specific tool for this job does exist, but is only available for purchase in local stores.

SERVES 4 TO 6

275g/10oz stale, hard bread, finely grated
150g/5oz freshly grated Parmesan cheese
8 eggs
grated rind of 1 unwaxed lemon
freshly grated nutmeg
a little milk, as required
about 2 litres/3½ pints/9 cups strong chicken stock
sea salt and ground black pepper

1 Put the grated bread, Parmesan cheese, eggs and lemon rind in a bowl and mix together with your hands to form a thick paste.

2 Season with nutmeg, salt and pepper. If the mixture is too crumbly, dampen with a little milk. Leave to rest in the refrigerator, covered, for 1 hour.

3 Bring the stock to a gentle boil in a large pan. Using a ricer or food mill with large holes, push the bread mixture, a small amount at a time, into the hot stock, cutting off the strands to drop into the soup when they are about 10cm/4in long.

4 Cook for 5–6 minutes and then serve hot.

PER PORTION Energy 188kcal/785kJ; Protein 16.5g; Carbohydrate 6.9g, of which sugars 0.9g; Fat 8.9g, of which saturates 5.3g; Cholesterol 38mg; Calcium 327mg; Fibre 1.2g; Sodium 290mg.

TUSCAN BEAN AND CABBAGE SOUP
LA RIBOLLITA

An absolutely classic Tuscan recipe, la ribollita is typical of the big, wholesome soups of this region. When in season, cavolo nero, the narrow-leafed black cabbage of Tuscany, is used for this dish, but in fact any kind of cabbage will work just as well. At the table, offer around olive oil so that people can drizzle it over their individual portions, as they wish – this is known as blessing your soup in Tuscany. You can also offer freshly grated Parmesan or aged Pecorino cheese.

SERVES 4 TO 6

- 250g/9oz stale country-style white or brown bread, sliced
- 30ml/2 tbsp olive oil, plus extra to serve
- 3 carrots, coarsely chopped
- 2 potatoes, peeled and cubed
- 2 garlic cloves, finely chopped
- 2 onions, finely sliced
- 1 small cabbage, shredded
- 2–3 handfuls of any other leaf vegetables of your choice, such as spinach or chard, coarsely shredded
- 4 Italian pork or wild boar sausages
- about 1.2 litres/2 pints/5 cups cold water
- 150g/5oz/1 cup cooked cannellini beans (see Cook's Tips)
- sea salt and ground black pepper
- freshly grated Parmesan or Pecorino cheese, to serve (optional)

1 Season the stale bread with salt and pepper. Brush it thoroughly on either side with the olive oil. Use it to line a soup tureen or large heatproof bowl.

2 Put all the vegetables and the sausages into a large pan and cover with the cold water. Season with salt and pepper and cover with a lid. Bring to the boil, then reduce the heat and simmer for 1½ hours, stirring occasionally and adding water if the liquid reduces too much.

3 Remove the sausages and keep warm. Stir the beans into the soup and simmer for a further 10 minutes.

4 Adjust the seasoning to taste, then pour the soup over the prepared bread in the tureen or bowl. Arrange the sausages on top, then cover and leave to rest for about 10 minutes before serving. Serve with a jug (pitcher) of olive oil to drizzle over the soup, and Parmesan or Pecorino cheese, if you like.

COOK'S TIPS

- Very stale bread is best for this recipe.
- If using canned beans, rinse them thoroughly before using. If using dried beans, soak 50g/2oz/⅓ cup overnight in cold water, then rinse. Boil them for 5 minutes, drain and rinse. Return to the pan with fresh water. Boil gently until tender.

PER PORTION Energy 354kcal/1482kJ; Protein 11.5g; Carbohydrate 43.8g, of which sugars 12g; Fat 15.9g, of which saturates 4.9g; Cholesterol 16mg; Calcium 151mg; Fibre 5.8g; Sodium 617mg.

SERVES 4 TO 6

200g/7oz whole spelt grain
75g/3oz pancetta (smoked if possible), coarsely chopped
75ml/5 tbsp extra virgin olive oil
a few thyme sprigs
1 onion, finely sliced
2 garlic cloves, left whole
1.8kg/4lb ripe plum tomatoes, seeded and chopped, or 400g/14oz canned chopped tomatoes (with juice)
a handful of fresh flat leaf parsley leaves, chopped
a handful of fresh basil leaves, torn into small pieces
about 1 litre/1¾ pints/4 cups hot vegetable, chicken or meat stock
sea salt and ground black pepper
freshly grated Pecorino or Parmesan cheese, to serve

PER PORTION Energy 294kcal/1239kJ; Protein 7.1g; Carbohydrate 38.2g, of which sugars 10.1g; Fat 13.7g, of which saturates 2.6g; Cholesterol 8mg; Calcium 48mg; Fibre 3.6g; Sodium 189mg.

TUSCAN SPELT SOUP
ZUPPA DI FARRO

This hearty soup exists in many different forms and is especially common in the Garfagnana region, the mountainous area north-west of Lucca, but it is popular in the rest of Tuscany as well, including along the Umbrian border. Spelt is an ancient ingredient, and is reminiscent of an era when wheat was simply not available in these parts. Recently, it has become fashionable all over the country, and is used in soups such as this one, or boiled, drained, cooled and turned into delicious salads.

1 Wash the spelt well, picking over the grains to remove chaff, pebbles or bad grains, then soak it overnight in cold water. Rinse the soaked spelt repeatedly until the water runs clear.

2 Fry the pancetta gently in half the olive oil, until the fat runs, then add the thyme, onion and garlic. Cook for 5 minutes, or until the onion has softened.

3 Remove and discard the garlic. Stir in the chopped tomatoes, parsley and basil. Cook for 3 minutes.

4 Stir in the hot stock and bring back to the boil. Add the spelt.

5 Cook the soup over a low heat, stirring often, for about 2 hours, or until the spelt is cooked (test by tasting one grain: it should be tender).

6 Adjust the seasoning. Remove from the heat and leave the soup for 1 hour to serve it just warm, with the remaining olive oil drizzled over. Offer around some grated cheese for each person to add to their own portion.

CHICKPEA AND PORK SOUP
MINESTRA DI CECI E MAIALE

This dish, which originates from Le Marche, is one of those robust cold-weather soups that are designed to fill hungry stomachs in the depths of a bitter winter, where the only heating comes from the kitchen fireplace. Guaranteed to provide much sustenance and comfort, it is filling and satisfying, as well as wonderfully warming. Made with a variety of the most basic of local ingredients that are available to even the poorest of families, this soup, and many others like it, relies on long, gentle cooking to draw out the depth and mixture of flavours and to keep the meat from becoming stringy and tough.

SERVES 4 TO 6

275g/10oz/1½ cups dried chickpeas, soaked overnight and drained
45–60ml/3–4 tbsp extra virgin olive oil, plus extra to serve
200g/7oz prosciutto crudo, diced
2 garlic cloves, chopped
1 large onion, chopped
a large handful of fresh parsley leaves, chopped
3 pork ribs
200g/7oz escarole or bitter leaves, such as endive (US chicory)
3 celery sticks, coarsely chopped
225g/8oz passata (bottled strained tomatoes)
sea salt and ground black pepper
freshly grated Pecorino cheese and toasted crusty bread, thinly sliced, to serve

1 Rinse the drained chickpeas. Put them in a large pan and cover with plenty of water. Bring to the boil and boil hard for 5 minutes, then drain and rinse again.

2 Return the chickpeas to the pan and cover with fresh water. Bring to the boil and boil gently for 15 minutes.

3 Meanwhile, put the olive oil in a large pan or flameproof casserole and fry the prosciutto, garlic and onion until soft.

4 Add the fresh parsley and cook for 5 minutes.

5 Drain the chickpeas and add them to the pan. Stir well to allow the chickpeas to combine, then add 2 litres/3½ pints/9 cups water and simmer, covered, for about 1 hour.

6 Cut the meat from the pork ribs, and then cut it into rough chunks.

7 Bring the soup back to the boil and, as soon as it reaches boiling point, add the bitter leaves, celery, pork meat and bones to the pan.

8 Stir, then add the passata and season to taste with salt and pepper. Stir once more and cover tightly with a lid.

9 Leave the soup to simmer over the lowest possible heat for about 3 hours, stirring occasionally.

10 Adjust the seasoning to taste and serve with freshly grated Pecorino cheese, a drizzle of extra virgin olive oil and toasted bread.

COOK'S TIPS

- This soup is even more delicious served reheated the following day.
- You can use canned chickpeas, although the flavour will not be as intense.

PER PORTION Energy 302kcal/1268kJ; Protein 17.6g; Carbohydrate 31.2g, of which sugars 7.7g; Fat 12.8g, of which saturates 2.8g; Cholesterol 22mg; Calcium 118mg; Fibre 6.8g; Sodium 149mg.

STUFFED DEEP-FRIED GIANT OLIVES
OLIVE ALL'ASCOLANA

These stuffed olives are one of Le Marche's most famous and traditional recipes. They are usually served either as part of an antipasto or alongside a meat recipe as a delicious side dish. They are best served just warm, but are also good cold. The key to this recipe is to find olives that are large enough to stuff successfully without them splitting. The recipe is named after the town of Ascoli Piceno, which is surrounded on three sides by the mountains of two vast national parks: Parco Nazionale dei Monti Sibillini on the north-western flank and Parco Nazionale dei Monti della Laga to the south.

SERVES 6

60 giant green olives, preserved in brine
115g/4oz pork fat
60ml/4 tbsp extra virgin olive oil
150g/5oz/⅔ cup minced (ground) pork
115g/4oz/½ cup minced (ground) beef
15ml/1 tbsp tomato purée (paste), diluted in 15ml/1 tbsp cold water
3 chicken livers, trimmed and chopped
45ml/3 tbsp fresh white breadcrumbs
45ml/3 tbsp beef stock
1 egg, beaten
50g/2oz/⅔ cup freshly grated Parmesan cheese
pinch freshly grated nutmeg
75ml/5 tbsp plain (all-purpose) flour
2 eggs beaten with 15ml/1 tbsp milk
45–60ml/3–4 tbsp fine dry breadcrumbs
vegetable oil, for deep-frying
sea salt and ground black pepper
lemon wedges, to serve

1 Stone (pit) all the olives carefully using an olive pitter, cherry stoner, apple corer or long, thin-bladed knife. It is important to keep them whole and as tidy as possible. Discard the stones (pits).

2 In a frying pan, heat the pork fat with the oil, then add the minced pork and beef, and cook for about 5 minutes until the meat is all well browned.

3 Add the tomato purée mixture to the pan. Mix well, and cook for about 20 minutes, stirring occasionally.

4 Add the chicken livers and cook for a further 10 minutes.

5 Allow the mixture to cool, and then chop the liver and mince mixture finely using a heavy knife. Alternatively, put the liver and mince mixture into a food processor or blender and blend until smooth.

6 Add the breadcrumbs, stock, beaten egg and Parmesan cheese to the mixture. Add the nutmeg and season with salt and pepper.

7 Carefully, using your fingers, fill each olive with a little of the meat mixture.

8 Roll the olives in the flour, then in the beaten egg and milk, and then in the dry breadcrumbs.

9 Half fill a heavy pan with oil. If using a deep-fryer, fill it to the level recommended in the instruction book. Heat the oil to 180°C/350°F or until a cube of bread, added to the oil, turns golden in about 45 seconds.

10 Add the olives, in batches, to the hot oil and deep-fry until golden brown. Drain the olives on kitchen paper and serve hot or cold with the lemon wedges.

PER PORTION Energy 602kcal/2488kJ; Protein 18.2g; Carbohydrate 6.2g, of which sugars 0.5g; Fat 55.6g, of which saturates 15.8g; Cholesterol 210mg; Calcium 151mg; Fibre 1.2g; Sodium 983mg.

TUSCAN LIVER PÂTÉ
CROSTINI

Some say that this is the original, 15th-century recipe for pâté from the Medici kitchens, and that it was then exported to France along with various other classic recipes, such as onion soup and ice cream. It is a delicious way to sharpen the appetite at the start of a meal. In Tuscany the word crostini traditionally refers to this pâté, as opposed to toasted bread with various toppings, which is what the word has come to mean in more recent times.

SERVES 4

45ml/3 tbsp olive oil
40g/1½oz unsalted butter
½ onion, finely chopped
1 carrot, finely chopped
1 celery stick, finely chopped
15ml/1 tbsp finely chopped parsley
1 chicken liver, trimmed
115g/4oz calf's liver, trimmed
30ml/2 tbsp dry white wine
25ml/1½ tbsp tomato purée (paste), diluted in 60ml/4 tbsp hot water or stock
25g/1oz salted capers, rinsed and finely chopped
4 large or 8 small thin slices crusty white or brown bread
sea salt and ground black pepper

1 Put the olive oil and half the butter in a large pan and fry the vegetables over a medium heat for 15 minutes, or until soft.

2 Add the parsley, chicken and calf's livers. Stir well and add the dry white wine. Cook for 2 minutes, stirring, then add the diluted tomato purée.

3 Season to taste, then add 30ml/2 tbsp water, cover and simmer for about 20 minutes.

4 Remove from the heat, lift the livers out of the sauce and chop finely or process them in a food processor or blender until quite smooth.

5 Return the semi-puréed livers to the pan. Stir in the remaining butter and the capers. Heat through and remove from the heat, but keep warm.

6 Spread the bread generously with the liver topping and serve.

PER PORTION Energy 472kcal/1979kJ; Protein 16.6g; Carbohydrate 48.7g, of which sugars 4.8g; Fat 23.8g, of which saturates 8.3g; Cholesterol 177mg; Calcium 124mg; Fibre 2.2g; Sodium 596mg.

TUSCAN BREAD AND TOMATO SALAD
LA PANZANELLA

This famous Tuscan salad has a substantial bread base with the addition of tomatoes, onions, cucumbers and basil to give it flavour and freshness. Served elegantly, in a pretty bowl or on a flat platter, this makes a wonderful appetizer and can be enlarged with the addition of flaked canned tuna in olive oil or cooked fish fillets to make a more filling meal. It is a rustic dish, perfect for hot summer days, and is a useful way of using up precious leftover bread, which needs to be coarse and crusty.

1 Soak the bread in cold water for about 15 minutes, then squeeze the bread dry in a clean dish towel.

2 Mix the damp bread with the tomatoes, onion, cucumber and basil.

3 Dress the salad with with olive oil, vinegar and salt and pepper to taste.

4 Toss the salad ingredients together thoroughly and leave it to stand for about 30 minutes before serving.

SERVES 4

8 slices casareccio-type bread or ciabatta, stale
4 beefsteak tomatoes, chopped
1 large red onion, chopped
1 large cucumber, chopped
a handful of fresh basil leaves, torn into pieces
extra virgin olive oil, to taste
red wine vinegar, to taste
sea salt and ground black pepper

COOK'S TIP

Extra virgin olive oil is a premium oil with a superior flavour and is perfect for tasty salad dressings.

PER PORTION Energy 238kcal/998kJ; Protein 5.3g; Carbohydrate 28g, of which sugars 5.9g; Fat 12.5g, of which saturates 1.9g; Cholesterol 0mg; Calcium 116mg; Fibre 3.2g; Sodium 259mg.

TUSCAN BREAD FRITTERS
FICATTOLE

These simple and delicious little bread-dough fritters appear all over Tuscany under various different names, but the basic principle is always the same: just flour, salt, water and yeast are needed to make them, and plenty of hot olive oil for deep-frying them until they are crispy and golden brown. Perfect as a little snack, they are usually served with an antipasto platter as an alternative to ordinary bread. You might also come across them under the name of panzanelle, frittelle di pane, crescentine or many other locally used names. In some parts of Tuscany cooks add herbs such as fresh basil to the dough to add extra flavour. Serve them piping hot with cured meats such as salami, mortadella or prosciutto.

SERVES 4

300g/11oz/2⅔ cups plain (all-purpose) flour, plus extra for dusting
30g/1¼oz fresh yeast
120ml/4fl oz/½ cup warm water
300ml/½ pint/1¼ cups cold water
olive oil and sunflower oil mixed, for deep-frying (see Cook's Tip)
sea salt

1 Put the flour on to the work surface in a mound and make a hollow in the centre with your fist.

2 Mix the yeast with the warm water and a pinch of salt and stir until dissolved.

3 Work the yeast mixture into the flour, adding enough of the cold water to produce a smooth dough.

4 Knead for 10 minutes, or until soft and spongy. Put the ball of dough into a lightly oiled bowl and cover with oiled clear film (plastic wrap).

5 Leave to rise in a warm place for about 1 hour, or until it has doubled in size.

6 Knock back (punch down) the dough and roll it out on a floured surface. Cut into finger-sized strips.

7 Heat the olive and sunflower oils in a deep-fryer or large, deep pan until a small piece of dough, dropped into the oil, sizzles instantly.

8 Fry the fritters, in batches, for 2–3 minutes, or until golden brown.

9 Remove the fritters carefully from the oil using a slotted spoon. Drain the fritters thoroughly on kitchen paper and sprinkle with salt. Serve immediately.

COOK'S TIP

Do make sure the oil is really hot before you start to deep-fry the fritters. On this occasion the perfect oil would be olive oil, but not extra virgin, mixed approximately half and half with a seed oil such as sunflower.

PER PORTION Energy 604kcal/2518kJ; Protein 9.3g; Carbohydrate 58.5g, of which sugars 1.1g; Fat 38.5g, of which saturates 5.4g; Cholesterol 0mg; Calcium 110mg; Fibre 2.3g; Sodium 6mg.

ROSEMARY AND SULTANA ROLLS
PANINI AL RAMERINO

These deliciously fragrant little rolls, slightly sweetened with juicy sultanas, are a perfect teatime treat and have always been popular with children. Served warm, with olive oil, butter or a sour cheese such as a Stracchino, they are wonderful with a fresh glass of milk or hot chocolate. Alternatively, try them with salami, olives, prosciutto crudo or mortadella as an antipasto. However they are served, the intense rosemary perfume, released as their crusts are broken, will transport you to Tuscany in an instant.

1 Soak the sultanas in warm water for 10 minutes, then drain and dry thoroughly on kitchen paper. Grease a large baking sheet.

2 Put the bread dough on the work surface and make a hollow in the centre.

3 Heat the oil (do not allow it to sizzle) in a small pan with the rosemary leaves for 10 minutes. Cool completely, then pour the oil into the hollow in the dough.

4 Knead together for 10 minutes, then roll the dough into a ball and place it in a lightly oiled bowl. Cover with oiled clear film (plastic wrap) and put in a warm place to rise for 1 hour.

5 Knead the sultanas into the dough. With oiled hands, shape the dough into 14 small rounded rolls. Place on the baking sheet, cover with oiled clear film and leave to rise for 45 minutes, or until doubled in size. Preheat the oven to 200°C/400°F/Gas 6.

6 Bake the rolls for 10 minutes, or until crisp and golden. Serve warm or cold.

MAKES 14 SMALL ROLLS

450g/1lb ready-made, risen Basic Bread Dough
60ml/4 tbsp good-quality extra virgin olive oil, plus extra for greasing
1 rosemary sprig, leaves coarsely chopped
30ml/2 tbsp sultanas (golden raisins)

PER PORTION Energy 110kcal/463kJ; Protein 2.8g; Carbohydrate 17.3g, of which sugars 2.3g; Fat 3.8g, of which saturates 0.6g; Cholesterol 0mg; Calcium 37mg; Fibre 0.5g; Sodium 168mg.

MAKES 2 OR 3 LARGE LOAVES

225g/5lb 6oz ready-made, risen Basic Bread Dough
about 725g/1lb 9oz/6¼ cups strong white bread flour
warm water, as needed
115g/4oz pork dripping
4 eggs, beaten
10g/¼oz fresh yeast mixed with 75ml/5 tbsp warm water
275g/10oz/1⅔ cups freshly grated Pecorino cheese
45–60ml/3–4 tbsp extra virgin olive oil
sea salt and ground black pepper
unsalted butter, for greasing
plain (all-purpose) flour, for dusting

UMBRIAN EASTER BREAD
PIZZA DI PASQUA AL FORMAGGIO

This is not a pizza as such, but is called a pizza since the word is sometimes used to describe a savoury bread, or a simple cake. It is actually very rich and labour-intensive, which is typical of the traditional dishes that mark the feasting for important religious festivities. In Italy, Easter Monday is often the day when family and friends head into the countryside for a picnic, and this bread would be exactly the kind of food to take along to share on such an occasion. Serve with cured meats, olives and cheeses.

1 Knead the bread dough with 500g/1¼lb/5 cups of the flour and enough warm water to achieve a very soft dough.

2 Turn this dough into a lightly oiled bowl and cover with lightly oiled clear film (plastic wrap). Leave in a warm place to rise for about 1 hour, or until doubled in size.

3 Knead the pork dripping, eggs, yeast mixture, Pecorino cheese, olive oil and salt and pepper into the dough.

4 Knead thoroughly, using the remaining 225g/8oz/2 cups strong white bread flour, to achieve a dough that is not too sticky.

5 Butter and flour two or three large loaf tins (pans). Divide the dough among the tins. Leave in a warm place to rise for 2 hours.

6 Preheat the oven to 200°C/400°F/Gas 6 and bake the bread for 50 minutes, until the top of the loaves are golden brown and crisp. Cool completely before removing them from the tins.

COOK'S TIP

You could bake the dough in terracotta pots instead.

PER LOAF Energy 2030kcal/8543kJ; Protein 79.8g; Carbohydrate 261.7g, of which sugars 7.5g; Fat 81.3g, of which saturates 37.6g; Cholesterol 381mg; Calcium 1642mg; Fibre 9.7g; Sodium 1881mg.

PASTA, GNOCCHI, RICE AND POLENTA

PASTA, GNOCCHI, RISO E POLENTA

In Tuscany, Umbria and Le Marche, just as almost anywhere in Italy, the primo – or first course – is without question the most important course of the whole meal and it comes in countless forms. It could be a steaming dish of pasta served with a sauce, known as pastasciutta, which is a quintessential dish of Italian cooking. Rice plays a much smaller part in the local cuisine, but nevertheless, a handful of risotto and rice recipes are usually present on menus, especially in Tuscany. Hearty, ribsticking polenta, usually associated with the very north of the country, also plays a significant part in the cuisine of these regions. It can often constitute a meal in itself, rather than being served as a primo, as it is so wonderfully sustaining. Gnocchi, or dumplings, also have a place here, especially the delicate spinach variety that are made to an ancient Florentine recipe.

HEARTY STAPLES AND DELICATE DUMPLINGS

The recipes contained in this chapter represent what is traditionally considered to be the first course of the meal. However, in these days of smaller appetites, it is not uncommon in many Italian households for a pasta, risotto or polenta dish to be served with an accompanying vegetable dish or a salad, as a main course, followed by fruit or a light dessert, removing the antipasto and the secondo altogether. Lengthy, formal meals with many different courses are now reserved for special occasions, such as weddings or huge family gatherings.

A pasta sauce can be ingeniously simple, such as extra virgin olive oil with garlic and black pepper, or luxurious and rich, made with meat, vegetables or fish. Pasta is surprisingly versatile – it can be stuffed or baked as well as boiled. Fresh pasta has its origins in the neighbouring region of Emilia Romagna, so it is no wonder that this tradition has spilled over into Tuscany, Le Marche and, to a lesser extent, Umbria. As well as dishes made with fresh egg pasta, such as the fantastic Marche Baked Pasta, these regions also boast many recipes using dried durum wheat pasta, such as Spaghetti with Wild Asparagus.

Gnocchi are not actually a type of pasta, but small dumplings, which are made with an intriguing assortment of ingredients throughout Italy, from semolina and polenta to potato and pumpkin. In Tuscany, the much-loved, classic version is made using spinach.

Risotto and polenta, traditionally an integral part of the cuisine of the far north of Italy, also appear in Tuscany, Umbria and Le Marche. Polenta, a very simple dish, represents the basic traditions of peasant cuisine. Risotto, traditionally a more sophisticated dish, is celebrated with rich local ingredients, such as robust Chianti or wild mushrooms.

PASTA AND CHICKPEAS
PASTA E CECI

This simple, thick pasta soup, comprised of the very cheapest of ingredients, is made all over Italy with few variations on the central theme. It is intended to be a satisfying, cheap, nourishing and tasty soup that relies on the addition of other available ingredients to enrich and improve on the basic recipe. You could easily, for example, use rich chicken or meat stock instead of water, or add some meaty bones to the simmering soup, or you could add other vegetables, such as shredded cabbage, ripe tomatoes or chopped courgettes (zucchini), towards the end of cooking. Very much the same recipe can be used and adapted if making a basic pasta e fagioli (pasta and beans) or pasta e lenticchie (pasta and lentils).

1 Rinse the drained chickpeas. Put them in a large pan and cover with plenty of water. Bring to the boil and boil hard for 5 minutes, then drain and rinse again.

2 Return the chickpeas to the pan, cover with fresh water and add the vegetables and rosemary sprigs. Bring to the boil and simmer gently for 45 minutes. Remove and discard the vegetables.

3 Whiz one-third of the chickpeas in a blender or food processor until smooth, then return to the pan. Stir, season and simmer for 20 minutes.

4 Cook the pasta in a pan of salted boiling water until almost tender. Drain the pasta, stir it into the chickpeas, then boil everything for about a minute, stirring gently. Adjust the seasoning, and serve. Offer olive oil to diners to drizzle over their soup.

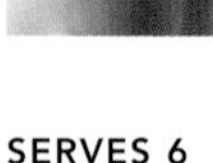

SERVES 6

1kg/2¼lb dried chickpeas, soaked overnight and drained
2 celery sticks
2 carrots
2 onions, peeled and halved
4 garlic cloves
2 x 15cm/6in sprigs fresh rosemary
450g/1lb short ribbed pasta, such as ditalini
sea salt and ground black pepper
extra virgin olive oil, to serve

PER PORTION Energy 820kcal/3477kJ; Protein 45.4g; Carbohydrate 144.9g, of which sugars 12.2g; Fat 10.6g, of which saturates 1g; Cholesterol 0mg; Calcium 310mg; Fibre 21.6g; Sodium 83mg.

SERVES 6

- 60ml/4 tbsp olive oil
- 2 garlic cloves, peeled and left whole
- 900g/2lb fresh wild asparagus, fine local asparagus or sprue, cut into short sections
- 450g/1lb ripe tomatoes, peeled, seeded and chopped
- 450g/1lb spaghetti
- sea salt and ground black pepper
- freshly grated Parmesan cheese, to serve

PER PORTION Energy 373kcal/1572kJ; Protein 13.9g; Carbohydrate 60.9g, of which sugars 7.7g; Fat 9.8g, of which saturates 1.4g; Cholesterol 0mg; Calcium 65mg; Fibre 5.5g; Sodium 11mg.

SPAGHETTI WITH WILD ASPARAGUS
SPAGHETTI CON ASPARAGI DI CAMPO

The secret of this recipe is in the simplicity of just a few carefully-selected ingredients. All along the mountains and hillsides that cross Umbria you can find small wild asparagus that is famous for its amazingly bright green colour and its intense flavour. This delicious wild vegetable, which the local people go out to pick on warm spring days when it is in season, is used to make this local speciality. Good-quality, fresh asparagus, or sprue, which are the first pickings and have thinner stems, can of course be used in the place of the famous wild Umbrian asparagus.

1 Heat the olive oil in a pan and fry the garlic gently until golden brown. Discard the garlic. Add the asparagus to the garlic-flavoured oil. Stir and cook gently for about 5 minutes, until tender.

2 Add the tomatoes to the asparagus and stir together. Season to taste.

3 Cook the spaghetti in a large pan of salted boiling water, until al dente. Drain and return to the pan.

4 Pour the asparagus sauce over the pasta and mix together gently. Transfer to a warm serving dish and serve immediately, with the Parmesan cheese offered separately.

RAVIOLI IN THE PESARO STYLE

RAVIOLI PESARESI

Ravioli with a ricotta cheese and spinach filling exist in most parts of Italy where fresh pasta is featured. There are many variations on this recipe – meat or other kinds of cheese can be added to the filling mixture, and instead of spinach, Swiss chard can be used, or it could even be substituted by fresh young nettles. In Le Marche, it is the addition of lots of tangy lemon rind that gives a fresh boost to the flavour. Lemons grown in the coastal areas of Italy always have an especially recognizable intensity of perfume and taste.

SERVES 6

about 400g/14oz/3½ cups plain (all-purpose) flour
50g/2oz/2 tbsp fine semolina, plus extra for dusting
4 eggs
1 egg yolk
350g/12oz fresh ricotta cheese
500g/1¼lb spinach, cooked and finely chopped
grated rind of 1 large unwaxed lemon
115g/4oz/1¼ cups freshly grated mild Pecorino cheese
sea salt and ground black pepper
Basic Tomato Sauce or melted butter, to serve

1 Mix together the flour and semolina and place the mixture on a work surface in a mound. Use your fist to make a hollow in the centre.

2 Beat the eggs and egg yolk together and pour the mixture into the hollow in the flour. Work the flour and eggs together with your fingertips until you have a pliable ball of dough that is neither too sticky or too dry – add more flour as required.

3 Knead the ball of dough until it is smooth and elastic. Cover with a clean cloth or wrap in clear film (plastic wrap), and leave to rest for about 30 minutes while you make the filling for the ravioli.

4 In a large bowl, mix together the ricotta cheese, chopped spinach and grated lemon rind. Season to taste with salt and pepper.

5 Roll out the pasta into a long, thin rectangle as finely and as evenly as possible. Drop the filling, in a neat row, along half the sheet of pasta, a scant tablespoon at a time, leaving about 2.5cm/1in between the little mounds of filling. Fold the sheet over to cover the filling.

6 With your fingers, press down firmly between the mounds of filling so that the pasta sticks together and closes up like a little parcel. Cut out the ravioli with a serrated pasta cutter or knife and press round the edges again to make sure each is perfectly sealed.

7 Dust a wide baking tray with semolina and lay the ravioli over it, taking care not to overlap them or lay them on top of one another.

8 Bring a large pan of water to the boil and drop in the ravioli. Cook for 3–4 minutes, in batches. They should rise to the surface when cooked. Scoop out the ravioli using a large slotted spoon as soon as they are cooked and transfer them to a warmed bowl.

9 Dress the ravioli with tomato sauce or melted butter and sprinkle with freshly grated mild Pecorino cheese.

PER PORTION Energy 513kcal/2155kJ; Protein 26.3g; Carbohydrate 61.2g, of which sugars 3.8g; Fat 19.8g, of which saturates 10g; Cholesterol 201mg; Calcium 489mg; Fibre 4g; Sodium 377mg.

COOK'S TIP

The best place to make, knead and roll out pasta is on a wooden kitchen table or warm work surface. Marble is not suitable.

SERVES 4

- 120ml/4fl oz/½ cup olive oil
- 1 garlic clove
- a pinch of crushed chilli flakes
- 450g/1lb cuttlefish, cleaned and cut into small cubes
- 275g/10oz raw shrimp tails or prawns (shrimp), peeled and cut into small cubes
- 175ml/6fl oz/¾ cup dry white wine
- 3 ripe tomatoes, peeled, seeded and diced
- 350g/12oz fresh tagliatelle
- sea salt
- a handful of fresh flat leaf parsley, leaves chopped, to garnish

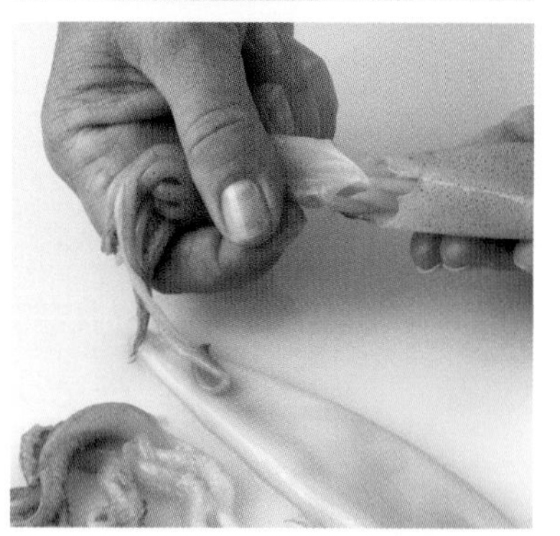

TAGLIATELLE WITH CUTTLEFISH AND SHRIMP
TAGLIATELLE CON CALAMARI E MOLECHE

The tails of the local shrimps are called moleche or molecche in the coastal areas of Le Marche, and are much sought after and greatly appreciated for their delicious sweetness. This is a very simple combination of tastes and textures, put together to create a sumptuous pasta dish. Using empty, clean scallop shells – known locally as scrigno di Venere (Venus's casket) – is one way in which pasta dishes such as this one often get served in Le Marche and also further south along the same coastline in the Abbruzzi. It looks pretty, and the pasta stays wonderfully hot.

1 Put the olive oil, garlic clove and chilli flakes into a pan and fry gently until the garlic is golden brown.

2 Add the cuttlefish and shrimp tails or prawns, and stir together.

3 Add the white wine, bring to the boil and cook for 1–2 minutes.

4 Add the diced tomatoes and stir well. Simmer for 5 minutes and season with salt.

5 Meanwhile, cook the tagliatelle in a large pan of salted boiling water until al dente.

6 Drain the pasta and return it to the pan. Add the sauce and mix together gently. Serve immediately, sprinkled with the fresh parsley.

PER PORTION Energy 630kcal/2654kJ; Protein 41.3g; Carbohydrate 67.4g, of which sugars 5.5g; Fat 20.5g, of which saturates 3g; Cholesterol 258mg; Calcium 152mg; Fibre 3.3g; Sodium 558mg.

WILD BOAR MALTAGLIATI IN THE AREZZO STYLE
MALTAGLIATI AL SUGO DI CINGHIALE ALL'ARETINA

Tuscany can stake a claim to just two different pasta shapes: pappardelle and maltagliati. Neighbouring Emilia Romagna is the most important region in the entire country when it comes to fresh pasta and its traditions, notably tagliatelle, ravioli and tortellini. In a gesture of typical Tuscan defiance, making pasta that is so obviously big and substantial, devoid of unnecessary ornament and, in the case of the maltagliati, cut roughly into rectangles, is testament to the ongoing feuding between the two areas. When it comes to food, Tuscany has to make a point of showing off. Cinghiale (wild boar) is one of the most iconic of all the Tuscan specialities.

SERVES 6

60ml/4 tbsp olive oil
1 onion, finely chopped
1 carrot, finely chopped
1 celery stick, finely chopped
115g/4oz prosciutto crudo, coarsely chopped
450g/1lb wild boar stewing meat, cubed
300ml/½ pint/1¼ cups full-bodied red wine
75ml/5 tbsp tomato purée (paste) diluted with 90ml/6 tbsp hot game or beef stock
275g/10oz canned tomatoes, strained
large pinch of fennel seeds
small pinch of ground cumin or cumin seed
450g/1lb maltagliati
sea salt and ground black pepper
freshly grated Parmesan cheese, to serve (optional)

1 Put the olive oil in a pan and fry the vegetables and prosciutto gently for 5 minutes, or until the onion is translucent.

2 Add the cubes of boar. Cook until browned all over, then pour over the wine and add seasoning. Cover and simmer for 1 hour.

3 Add half the diluted tomato purée and half the canned tomatoes to the meat and vegetable mixture. Cook for 1 hour more.

4 Add the remaining purée and tomatoes.

5 When the meat is falling apart, stir in the fennel seeds and cumin. Cover and simmer for a further 1 hour. Adjust the seasoning.

6 Bring a large pan of salted water to the boil, add the maltagliati, stir and then return to the boil. Cook according to the pack instructions, until al dente. Drain and return it to the pan.

7 Add the wild boar sauce to the pasta. Mix it through gently and transfer to a serving platter or individual plates to serve. Offer Parmesan cheese separately.

PER PORTION Energy 539kcal/2268kJ; Protein 30.8g; Carbohydrate 62.2g, of which sugars 8.7g; Fat 16.6g, of which saturates 4.3g; Cholesterol 55mg; Calcium 49mg; Fibre 3.9g; Sodium 327mg.

MARCHE BAKED PASTA
VINCISGRASSI

This wonderful dish is related distantly to the lasagna dish of Emilia Romagna, but it was created locally in honour of General Wiensgratz, the ruler of this area during the Austro-Hungarian domination of these northern provinces. The original recipe is more intricate, contains no tomato sauce and uses pigeon breasts. The pasta dough in the classic recipe uses Marsala mixed into the flour with the eggs, giving it a strange colour and quite a different taste. Here is a more modern version of the recipe, where arguably the most essential ingredient is still very much present: fresh black truffle.

SERVES 6 TO 8

200g/7oz/1¾ cups plain (all-purpose) flour
115g/4oz semolina
5 eggs
15ml/1 tbsp olive oil
a pinch of salt

FOR THE RAGÙ
45ml/3 tbsp olive oil
1 large onion, finely chopped
1 carrot, finely chopped
1 celery stick, finely chopped
a pinch of dried marjoram
225g/8oz stewing veal, coarsely minced (ground) or finely chopped
50g/2oz prosciutto crudo or pancetta, chopped
25g/1oz/½ cup dried porcini mushrooms, soaked for 30 minutes in boiling water until softened, then drained and chopped
15ml/1 tbsp plain (all-purpose) flour
250ml/8fl oz/1 cup red wine
1.5ml/¼ tsp freshly grated nutmeg
200ml/7fl oz/scant 1 cup thick passata (bottled strained tomatoes)
115g/4oz chicken livers, trimmed
65g/2½oz unsalted butter, plus extra for greasing
1 fresh black truffle, brushed clean and thinly sliced (see Cook's Tip)
600ml/1 pint/2½ cups White Sauce
150g/5oz/1½ cups freshly grated Parmesan cheese
sea salt and ground black pepper

COOK'S TIP

If you can't find a fresh black truffle, use truffle butter mixed into the White Sauce.

1 Mix together the flour and semolina, and pile on a work surface in a mound. Make a hollow in the centre with your fist.

2 Break the eggs into a bowl. Beat together with the oil and salt. Pour into the hollow in the flour, then work the flour and egg mixture together with your fingertips to form a pliable dough. Knead until springy, then wrap in clear film (plastic wrap), and leave to rest for 30 minutes.

3 Roll out the pasta dough using a rolling pin or pasta machine, and cut it into 18–20cm/7–8in squares or into rectangles. Drop the pasta into salted boiling water in batches and cook until soft, then drain on damp dish towels taking care not to overlap the pieces of pasta.

4 To make the ragù, put the oil in a pan and gently fry three-quarters of the onion with the carrot, celery and marjoram for 5 minutes, until the vegetables are softened but not coloured. Add the veal, prosciutto and porcini mushrooms, and cook gently until browned.

5 Add the flour and stir together lightly. Increase the heat, add the red wine and stir over a high heat for 1–2 minutes, or until the alcohol has evaporated from the wine. Lower the heat and season with the salt, pepper and nutmeg.

6 Add the passata and stir. Cover the pan and simmer gently for about 50 minutes, stirring occasionally.

7 Sauté the chicken livers in a pan with 15g/½oz/1 tbsp of the butter and the remaining onion until just browned. Slice thinly. Add the cooked chicken livers and the truffle to the ragù. Preheat the oven to 180°C/350°F/Gas 4.

8 Butter an ovenproof dish and cover the base with the pasta. Cover with the ragù, then a layer of White Sauce. Continue until you have used up all the ingredients, finishing with a layer of pasta. Cover with Parmesan cheese and dot with the remaining butter.

9 Bake for 30–40 minutes, until golden and bubbling. Leave to stand for at least 5 minutes before serving.

PER PORTION Energy 474kcal/1984kJ; Protein 25.3g; Carbohydrate 33.2g, of which sugars 2.7g; Fat 24.9g, of which saturates 11.2g; Cholesterol 232mg; Calcium 297mg; Fibre 1.7g; Sodium 488mg.

TUSCAN SPINACH GNOCCHI
MALFATTI

The word malfatti means 'badly made', so in other words they can look quite roughly shaped, without too much concern for elegant presentation. There is another version of this dish, which uses ricotta cheese as an ingredient as well as the spinach, but this is reputedly the much older recipe from the Medici kitchens. Malfatti are traditionally served simply with melted, warm, unsalted butter, but they can also be served with a basic tomato sauce. The recipe, in very similar versions, exists in various parts of the country, including the Veneto, but this is the most classically Tuscan version.

1 Steam or boil the spinach for 1–2 minutes until soft. Drain and leave to cool. Squeeze out the water, then chop finely. Put the spinach in a large bowl and stir in the eggs and egg yolks, then the cream.

2 Squeeze the bread dry with your hands, then mix it into the spinach with half the Parmesan. Season to taste with nutmeg, salt and pepper. Bring a large pan of water to the boil.

3 Using your fingers and a very light touch (see Cook's Tip), form the mixture into small dumplings, using a small amount of flour to prevent sticking.

4 Transfer the dumplings carefully, in small batches, into the boiling water. Cook the gnocchi for no more than 2–3 minutes – they will be ready when they float freely on the surface of the water.

5 Carefully remove the cooked gnocchi from the water using a slotted spoon and arrange them on a warmed serving dish. Continue in this way, with the remaining batches, until all the gnocchi are cooked.

6 Smother the gnocchi with the melted butter, sprinkle over the remaining Parmesan cheese and serve immediately.

SERVES 6

- 1.3kg/3lb fresh spinach
- 2 eggs, beaten
- 2 egg yolks
- 30ml/2 tbsp single (light) cream
- 150g/5oz stale bread, soaked in milk to cover for ½ hour
- 150g/5oz/1½ cups freshly grated Parmesan cheese
- 1.5ml/¼ tsp freshly grated nutmeg
- up to 75ml/5 tbsp plain (all-purpose) flour
- 115g/4oz unsalted butter, melted
- sea salt and ground black pepper

COOK'S TIP

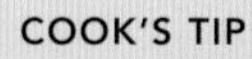

One way to achieve lightness when shaping the gnocchi, is to roll each ball of dough around a glass tumbler, dusted inside with flour. This way, you will prevent the gnocchi from becoming too solid and avoid squashing the air out.

PER PORTION Energy 465kcal/1933kJ; Protein 22.5g; Carbohydrate 25.7g, of which sugars 4.3g; Fat 30.8g, of which saturates 17.5g; Cholesterol 202mg; Calcium 738mg; Fibre 5.3g; Sodium 879mg.

SERVES 4

50g/2oz/1 cup dried porcini mushrooms
1 large onion, thinly sliced
115g/4oz/½ cup unsalted butter, plus extra for greasing
50ml/2fl oz/¼ cup olive oil
275g/10oz stewing pork, cubed
15ml/1 tbsp tomato purée (paste)
300ml/½ pint/1¼ cups pork or chicken stock
450g/1lb polenta flour
75ml/5 tbsp freshly grated Parmesan cheese
sea salt

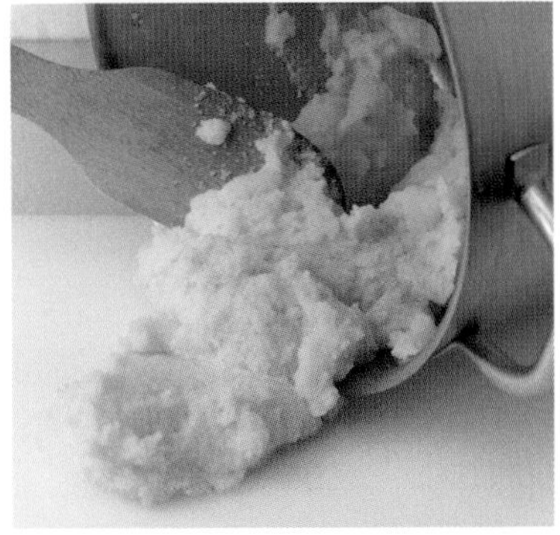

POLENTA GNOCCHI
GNOCCHI DI POLENTA

This is a tremendously substantial dish, which is perfect for cold, damp winter Tuscan days. It is a real rib-sticker, so if you decide to serve it make sure the next course is light. Polenta, like pasta, is hearty and sustaining, and it is an inexpensive way to satisfy hungry stomachs. The pork and porcini sauce can also be used to dress pasta or even as a risotto base.

1 Put the mushrooms in a bowl and cover with warm water. Allow to soak for about 15 minutes. Meanwhile, fry the onion in half the butter and the olive oil for 5 minutes, or until softened.

2 Add the stewing pork and stir thoroughly to brown the meat all over. Stir the tomato purée into the stock, then pour into the pan. Drain the mushrooms and chop them coarsely. Add them to the pan, stir and simmer for 20 minutes.

3 Meanwhile, bring 2 litres/3½ pints/9 cups water in a pan to the boil and add a large pinch of salt. Trickle the polenta flour into the water in a steady stream, whisking constantly.

4 Turn the heat to medium-low. Using a strong wooden spoon, stir the polenta constantly for 45 minutes, until it comes away from the sides of the pan. Turn the cooked polenta out on to a board and leave it to cool enough to set slightly.

5 Preheat the oven to 190°C/375°C/Gas 5. Butter a large ovenproof dish. Using a tablespoon dipped into cold water, scoop the polenta into balls and use to line the base of the dish. Cover with a little of the pork, dot with some of the butter and sprinkle with Parmesan. Continue layering the polenta, meat, butter and cheese, and finish with polenta coated in butter and cheese. Bake for 15–20 minutes. Serve.

PER PORTION Energy 878kcal/3654kJ; Protein 33.4g; Carbohydrate 84g, of which sugars 1.3g; Fat 44.4g, of which saturates 21.5g; Cholesterol 128mg; Calcium 244mg; Fibre 2.9g; Sodium 478mg.

POLENTA AND BEANS
POLENTA E FAGIOLI

Polenta and beans, a peasant-food staple, is eaten in all three regions, although this is an Umbrian recipe. This dish is made with standard polenta – cornmeal boiled in salted water until thick and porridge-like in consistency – to which some beans, enriched with tomato sauce, are added. The incorporation of the stewed beans and their sauce into the polenta makes for a really tasty dish. It is traditionally served with a good sprinkling of freshly grated Pecorino cheese.

1 Rinse the soaked beans. Put them in a large pan and cover with plenty of water. Bring to the boil and boil hard for 5 minutes, then drain and rinse again. Return the beans to the pan, cover with fresh water, bring to the boil, and boil gently for 45 minutes, or until softened. Drain away most of the water.

2 In a separate pan, fry the lard, white cooking fat or pancetta with the carrot, celery and onion for 10 minutes, or until softened.

3 Add the tomatoes and stir together. Simmer until thickened and glossy, then season to taste.

4 Drain and add the boiled beans, stir to mix and simmer while you cook the polenta.

5 Bring 2 litres/3½ pints/9 cups water to the boil in a large pan. Add a large pinch of salt, then trickle the polenta flour into the boiling water in a steady stream, whisking constantly. Turn the heat to medium-low. Using a strong wooden spoon, stir the polenta constantly for about 40 minutes.

6 Add the beans and their sauce, reserving a little to serve, if you wish, and continue to stir and cook for a further 10 minutes. Serve sprinkled with Pecorino cheese and a drizzle of olive oil.

SERVES 6

- 400g/14oz/2⅔ cups dried borlotti or cannellini beans, soaked overnight and drained
- 50g/2oz/⅓ cup lard, white cooking fat or fatty pancetta, cubed
- 1 carrot, finely chopped
- 1 celery stick, finely chopped
- 1 onion, finely chopped
- 450g/1lb ripe tomatoes, peeled, seeded and coarsely chopped
- 300g/11oz/2⅓ cups coarse or medium-grade polenta flour
- sea salt and ground black pepper
- freshly grated Pecorino cheese and extra virgin olive oil, to serve

COOK'S TIP

Although for convenience you could use canned beans for this recipe, you will get a better flavour if you use dried beans.

PER PORTION Energy 458kcal/1926kJ; Protein 20.2g; Carbohydrate 70.4g, of which sugars 5.8g; Fat 11.1g, of which saturates 3.6g; Cholesterol 8mg; Calcium 82mg; Fibre 12.9g; Sodium 26mg.

SERVES 4

1 red onion, finely chopped
½ celery stick, finely chopped
75g/3oz/6 tbsp unsalted butter
3 fresh sage leaves, finely chopped
200g/7oz/1 cup arborio rice
750ml/1¼ pints/3 cups full-bodied Chianti red wine
about 550ml/18fl oz/2½ cups simmering beef, chicken or vegetable stock
50g/2oz/⅔ cup freshly grated Parmesan cheese
sea salt and ground black pepper

RISOTTO WITH CHIANTI
RISOTTO AL CHIANTI

Although risotto is not a typical dish of this region, there is a small area of rice production near the small town of Pontedera – where the world-famous factory of Piaggio is situated, home of the Vespa scooter and the remarkable three-wheeled Ape agricultural vehicle – so a few rice recipes do exist. This one is for a classic risotto, and uses the red wine of the Chianti area to reiterate its Tuscan authenticity. Sage is the herb of choice, but since rosemary is a common herb of this region, you could use that instead.

1 Fry the red onion and celery with half the butter and the sage for 5 minutes, or until the onion and celery are soft and translucent.

2 Add the rice and stir until all the grains are toasted, opaque and crackling hot. Do not let the rice or vegetables brown. Add about 150ml/¼ pint/⅗ cup red wine. Stir for 2 minutes, or until the wine has been absorbed and the alcohol has evaporated. (The smell will change when this has occurred.) Gradually add the rest of the wine, little by little and stirring constantly, until all the wine has been used up.

3 Start adding the hot stock, a ladleful at a time, stirring constantly and allowing the liquid to be absorbed before adding more.

4 When the risotto is creamy and velvety, but the rice grains are still firm to the bite, remove the pan from the heat and stir in the remaining butter and the Parmesan cheese. Season to taste and cover with a lid.

5 Leave to stand for 3–4 minutes, then stir once more and transfer to a warmed platter to serve.

COOK'S TIP

Keep an eye on your risotto in the last stages of cooking, as arborio rice has a tendency to overcook extremely quickly, and become mushy in a flash.

PER PORTION Energy 507kcal/2110kJ; Protein 9.3g; Carbohydrate 41.7g, of which sugars 1.4g; Fat 19.7g, of which saturates 12.7g; Cholesterol 56mg; Calcium 181mg; Fibre 0.3g; Sodium 299mg.

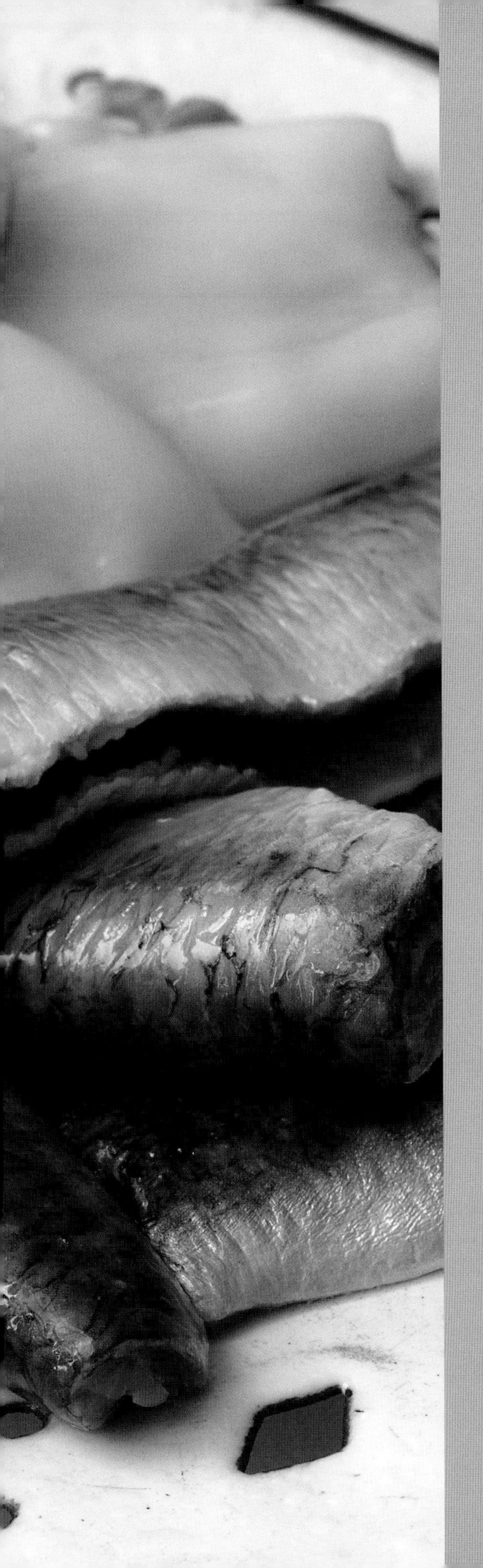

FISH AND SHELLFISH
PESCE E FRUTTI DI MARE

In the coastal regions of Tuscany to the west and Le Marche to the east, the catching and cooking of fresh seawater fish is very much a part of the local diet. In the coastal areas, both shellfish and crustaceans are highly prized and used to make many famous local dishes, either on their own or in addition to fresh fish. The freshness of the fish is absolutely paramount as far as the local cooks are concerned, and they like to buy their fish directly from the fishermen when they return to the harbour with their day's catch. Further inland, away from the sea, stoccafisso (stockfish or dried cod) and baccalà (salted cod) come into their own in a variety of recipes. Umbria, on the other hand, has many lakes, which yield a wide range of recipes using freshwater fish, such as perch, carp, tench and trout.

SALT COD, EELS AND SUSTAINING STEWS

Throughout Italy, fresh fish is cherished as an indispensable part of many meals and is treated with great respect and care. In Tuscany and Le Marche, all along the Tyrrhenian or Adriatic coast, the huge variety of locally caught seawater fish is used in a profusion of traditional recipes, forming a large part of the local menu. Markets always feature a superb selection of the day's catch, but it is also possible to buy fish straight from the boats in some small harbours.

In Tuscany, octopus plays a very important role and there are countless dishes created to celebrate this humble cephalopod. Mussels are also abundantly available and highly prized in this region, and are served in a sauce with pasta as well as on their own. Other shellfish, such as the tiny arselle that are gathered in square nets from the sandbars where the waves break, or the incredibly rare datteri di mare ('dates of the sea'), which are similar to mussels, are also considered to be a real delicacy. Inland, as well as the many recipes for stockfish (dried cod) or salted cod, locals enjoy catching and cooking eels from the marshy ditches on the flat plains.

Umbrian cooks have a wealth of recipes using freshwater fish, especially those caught in the waters of Lake Trasimeno. Fish forms an important part of the cuisine despite the region being landlocked.

In Le Marche, various kinds of fish are used in the different towns and villages strung along the coastline. Fresh fish is used where it is available, but away from the coastal towns preserved fish is used, such as canned tuna or salted cod.

Italians often gather friends and family together to prepare a meal entirely devoted to fish dishes, in order to celebrate this precious food.

STUFFED SARDINES
SARDINE RIPIENE

This delicious Tuscan recipe for fresh sardines or plump, overgrown anchovies could not be simpler and relies very much on the fish being freshly caught. Like many recipes from this region, the ingredients are quite generous and call for about ten fish per person, although you may prefer to reduce the quantities slightly. Once the fish have been filleted, any that have been damaged in the process are added to the bread filling. To remove the scales without them flying all over the kitchen, local cooks use a piece of newspaper – or yellow kitchen paper as found locally – soaked in water, to rub vigorously over the fish. They can be served just as they are, with a wedge of lemon, or with a basic tomato sauce flavoured with a pinch of ground fennel seeds.

1 Soak the bread in the milk to cover, then squeeze dry. Use any damaged fish fillets for the filling. Put all the perfectly shaped fillets to one side.

2 Mix the bread with the damaged fish, half the beaten eggs, the grated Parmesan cheese, garlic, parsley, chilli and a pinch of salt. Blend it all together to make a firm paste with your hands or a fork.

3 Sandwich two fillets together with a generous spoonful of the filling in the middle, then gently coat in the remaining beaten egg and then the flour. Repeat for the remaining fillets.

4 Heat the oil in large pan until sizzling, then fry the fish, in batches, until crisp and golden brown; about 2 minutes. Drain on kitchen paper and serve.

SERVES 4

2–3 stale crusty white bread rolls, crusts removed
about 120ml/4fl oz/½ cup milk
40 fresh sardines or large anchovies, scaled and filleted
3 eggs, beaten
45ml/3 tbsp freshly grated Parmesan cheese
2 garlic cloves, chopped
a handful of fresh flat leaf parsley, leaves chopped
1 dried red chilli
about 90ml/6 tbsp plain (all-purpose) flour
about 2 litres/3½ pints/9 cups sunflower oil, for deep-frying
sea salt

PER PORTION Energy 621kcal/2594kJ; Protein 35.8g; Carbohydrate 37.2g, of which sugars 2.6g; Fat 37.7g, of which saturates 9.3g; Cholesterol 155mg; Calcium 343mg; Fibre 1.3g; Sodium 505mg.

SERVES 4

1.2kg/2½lb fresh mackerel, cleaned
45ml/3 tbsp olive oil
6 small onions or shallots, chopped
4 carrots, chopped
1 large celery stick, chopped
a small handful of wild fennel fronds, chopped (see Cook's Tips)
a small bunch of fresh flat leaf parsley, leaves chopped
1 garlic clove, chopped
5cm/2in piece of unwaxed orange peel, chopped
juice of ½ orange
15ml/1 tbsp tomato purée (paste) diluted with 15ml/1 tbsp hot water or stock (see Cook's Tips)
sea salt and ground black pepper

MACKEREL WITH WILD FENNEL
SGOMBRI AL FINOCCHIELLO

Le Marche is a coastal region and fish plays an important part of the daily diet in the towns and villages that dot the shoreline. Fishermen and their families will generally eat their smaller catch, often salted to preserve it for longer, and will sell the larger and more profitable fish. Although mackerel isn't considered to be a much sought-after fish, it tastes superb when cooked with care and with some thoughtfully chosen ingredients, such as fennel.

1 Boil the mackerel in lightly salted water until cooked through (see Cook's Tips). Gently remove the cooked fish from the pan and fillet them carefully. Discard the bones, head and skin.

2 Put the oil in a large pan and gently fry the onions or shallots, carrots, celery, fennel, parsley, garlic and orange peel for 10 minutes. Season with salt and ground black pepper.

3 Add the orange juice. Stir and reduce the heat to low. Simmer, stirring frequently, for 15 minutes.

4 Stir in the diluted tomato purée. Cook for 15 minutes more, until the sauce has thickened.

5 Arrange the fish on a serving platter and pour over the sauce. Serve immediately, or chill to serve cold.

COOK'S TIPS

- Instead of wild fennel fronds, use fronds from a cultivated bulb, with 2.5ml/½ tsp ground fennel seeds for added flavour.
- To calculate the cooking time for boiling the fish, measure the thickest part and calculate 10 minutes per 2.5cm/1in.
- Save some of the water in which the mackerel was cooked to use as fish stock for diluting the tomato purée.

PER PORTION Energy 743kcal/3084kJ; Protein 57.7g; Carbohydrate 1.8g, of which sugars 1.4g; Fat 56g, of which saturates 11.1g; Cholesterol 159mg; Calcium 42mg; Fibre 0.4g; Sodium 189mg.

POLENTA WITH CANNED TUNA
POLENTA COL TONNO SOTT'OLIO

Creamy polenta is often served with rich sauces or stews, using meat, game or fish as the base. However, as a basic carbohydrate it can absorb and be combined with all kinds of different tastes and textures, in the same way that pasta, rice, potatoes or bread can. So, a can of best-quality tuna in olive oil, enlivened with the addition of a little tasty anchovy – either salted or preserved in oil – can be added to freshly made polenta for a sustaining meal. This is a recipe from Le Marche.

SERVES 2 TO 3

200g/7oz/¾ cup polenta flour
150g/5oz canned tuna in oil, flaked
2 salted anchovies, boned, or 4 anchovy fillets, rinsed
60ml/4 tbsp extra virgin olive oil
2–3 garlic cloves, chopped
a small handful of fresh flat leaf parsley leaves, chopped
a small handful of celery leaves, chopped
30ml/2 tbsp tomato purée (paste) diluted in 30ml/2 tbsp hot water or fish stock
sea salt and ground black pepper

1 First make the polenta. Bring 1.75 litres/3 pints/7½ cups water in a pan to the boil and add a large pinch of salt, then trickle the polenta flour into the water in a steady stream, whisking constantly.

2 Over a medium-low heat, using a strong wooden spoon, stir the polenta constantly for 45 minutes, or until it comes away from the sides of the pan.

3 Finely chop the tuna with the anchovies.

4 Put the oil in a pan and fry the garlic, parsley, celery leaves and fish together for 5 minutes. When the garlic is golden, stir in the diluted tomato purée. Season with pepper and simmer the sauce for about 30 minutes. Adjust the seasoning.

5 To serve, either turn the polenta out on a board, allow to set, cut into wedges and serve the sauce separately, or pour the soft polenta into individual bowls and add the fish topping to each.

PER PORTION Energy 484kcal/2018kJ; Protein 20.8g; Carbohydrate 50g, of which sugars 1.3g; Fat 21.8g, of which saturates 2.8g; Cholesterol 25mg; Calcium 19mg; Fibre 1.7g; Sodium 248mg.

RED MULLET IN THE STYLE OF LIVORNO
TRIGLIE ALLA LIVORNESE

The ancient port city of Livorno – Leghorn in English – is renowned for two famous fish specialities. One of these is the dense fish stew or soup called cacciucco, the other is this recipe for cooking sweet red mullet. The smaller the mullet, the better the flavour, but they are quite bony, so some people prefer to use large fillets rather than the whole fish – although the purists will claim that the flavour is nowhere near as delicious. It is particularly tasty if the fish is freshly caught.

SERVES 6

12 small red mullet, scaled, cleaned and gutted
30–45ml/2–3 tbsp plain (all-purpose) flour
75ml/5 tbsp olive oil
250ml/8fl oz/1 cup dry white wine
½ onion, finely chopped
1 garlic clove, chopped
1 bay leaf
a handful of fresh flat leaf parsley leaves, chopped
400g/14oz can tomatoes, strained and chopped
sea salt and ground black pepper

PER PORTION Energy 279kcal/1165kJ; Protein 24.9g; Carbohydrate 5.7g, of which sugars 2.9g; Fat 14.7g, of which saturates 1.4g; Cholesterol 0mg; Calcium 106mg; Fibre 0.9g; Sodium 133mg.

1 Dry the fish carefully inside and out with kitchen paper and coat them lightly with flour.

2 Heat the oil in a frying pan and fry the mullet for about 4 minutes.

3 Turn the fish over carefully, without breaking them, then add the wine, chopped onion, garlic, bay leaf, parsley and a little salt and pepper.

4 Shake the pan, then spoon the flavouring ingredients over the fish.

5 Allow the alcohol from the wine to evaporate for 1–2 minutes, then add the canned tomatoes.

6 Cover with a lid and simmer gently for a further 5 minutes. Serve immediately.

TUSCAN FISH STEW
CACCIUCCO

The story behind this traditional Tuscan fish stew, which originates from the port of Livorno, concerns a fisherman's wife whose husband was lost at sea during a storm. Left alone with many children to feed, she spent the little money she had left to buy fish for a soup called cacciucco, adding to the fish the few basic ingredients she had in her kitchen. So successful was the recipe that she managed to find work as a cook. To commemorate her, the soup is kept simple. Although it may vary slightly, it must contain at least five varieties of fresh fish, one for each of the 'C's in the recipe's name.

SERVES 6 TO 8

1.8kg/4lb assorted fish in varying sizes including some of the following: hake, monkfish, whiting, scorpion fish, moray eel, conger eel, John Dory, cleaned and gutted
450g/1lb octopus and cuttlefish or squid, cleaned
150ml/¼ pint/⅔ cup extra virgin olive oil
1 onion, chopped
1 carrot, chopped
1 celery stick, chopped
a handful of fresh flat leaf parsley leaves, finely chopped
1 dried red chilli, finely chopped
4 garlic cloves, 3 chopped and 1 halved
250ml/8fl oz/1 cup dry white wine
900g/2lb ripe tomatoes, peeled, seeded and coarsely chopped
12 large raw prawns (shrimp), peeled and deveined
15 small, thin slices of crusty white bread
sea salt and ground black pepper
about 1 litre/1¾ pints/4 cups simmering fish or vegetable stock, for basting and diluting

1 Cut the larger fish into generous pieces and leave the smaller ones whole. Keep all the heads, if removed, and set them aside. Cut the octopus and cuttlefish or squid into large pieces.

2 Put the oil in a large frying pan and fry the onion, carrot, celery, parsley, chilli and chopped garlic for 10 minutes, or until lightly golden.

3 Add the octopus and squid to the pan and cook for 2–3 minutes, or until they have released their fluid and it has been evaporated. Pour over the white wine. Cook for 2 minutes, until the alcohol has evaporated, then add the tomatoes. Stir and cover.

4 Simmer for 45 minutes, or until the squid and octopus are tender, then remove them and set aside. Add the fish heads and smaller fish to the pan and stir. Cook for about 25 minutes, basting occasionally with a little hot water or stock.

5 Pass the sauce and fish through the medium blade of a food mill (Mouli) and return to the pan. You should have a smooth, thick sauce. If it is too thick, dilute with a little hot water or stock.

6 Add the larger whole fish and pieces of fish to the pan and stir gently to coat with the sauce. Simmer together very gently for about 20 minutes.

7 Return the octopus and squid to the pan, and stir into the sauce. Add the prawns and cover with sauce, using more of the stock if necessary. Cook for about 15 minutes, until all the seafood is tender.

8 Meanwhile, toast the bread and rub with the halved garlic clove. Line the sides of a large bowl with the toast.

9 Raise the heat under the pan and stir the fish and sauce together while it returns to the boil. Season to taste with salt and pepper. Immediately, remove the pan from the heat and transfer the cacciucco to the bowl lined with toasted bread. Serve immediately.

PER PORTION Energy 585kcal/2458kJ; Protein 52.9g; Carbohydrate 46.8g, of which sugars 6.5g; Fat 19.8g, of which saturates 3.2g; Cholesterol 92mg; Calcium 168mg; Fibre 2.7g; Sodium 657mg.

UMBRIAN STUFFED GRILLED TROUT
TROTA AI FERRI

This is a very simple Umbrian recipe for trout. The region, being landlocked, relies on either freshwater fish from the rivers and lakes, or on preserved fish such as baccalà (salted cod) or canned fish. In Umbria, the trout caught in the river Nera are highly prized and much sought after. This recipe serves two people, so to feed more people you'll need a large barbecue.

1 Light the barbecue and wait until you have a heap of hot, even red embers. Position the grill rack. Rinse the trout under cold running water inside and out. Pat dry with kitchen paper.

2 In a small bowl, mix the breadcrumbs with the lemon juice, half the olive oil and the parsley and season to taste with salt and pepper.

3 Stuff the inside of each trout with this mixture. Score each trout lightly on each side through the skin, and rub the remaining oil all over the fish.

4 Lay the fish on a grill rack and cook for about 10 minutes on each side, until the trout is cooked through, brushing with more oil during the cooking process.

SERVES 2

2 medium sized trout, cleaned and gutted
120ml/8 tbsp soft breadcrumbs
juice of 1 lemon
150ml/10 tbsp extra virgin olive oil, plus extra for brushing
30ml/2 tbsp chopped fresh flat leaf parsley
sea salt and ground black pepper

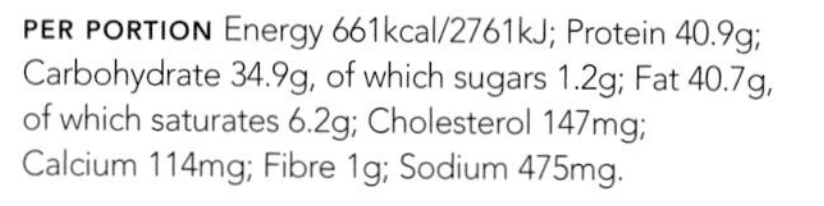

PER PORTION Energy 661kcal/2761kJ; Protein 40.9g; Carbohydrate 34.9g, of which sugars 1.2g; Fat 40.7g, of which saturates 6.2g; Cholesterol 147mg; Calcium 114mg; Fibre 1g; Sodium 475mg.

SERVES 6

1.25kg/2¾lb salted cod, soaked for 3 days, changing water frequently
1 egg
about 45ml/3 tbsp plain (all-purpose) flour
about 350ml/12fl oz/1½ cups cold water
about 2 litres/3½ pints/9 cups sunflower oil, for deep-frying

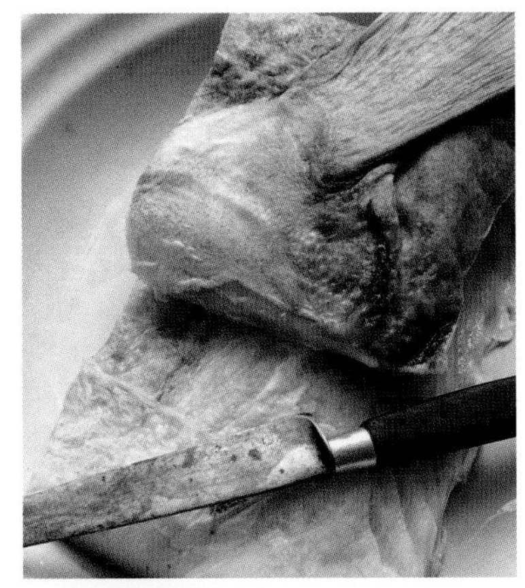

PER PORTION Energy 429kcal/1786kJ; Protein 39.9g; Carbohydrate 5.8g, of which sugars 0.1g; Fat 27.5g, of which saturates 3.1g; Cholesterol 128mg; Calcium 34mg; Fibre 0.2g; Sodium 137mg.

SALT COD FRITTERS
FRITTELLE DI BACCALÀ

As the region of Umbria has no coastline, the only fresh fish recipes found here will be those using the fish caught in the rivers, streams or lakes. Recipes for freshwater fish abound in the villages and towns surrounding Lake Trasimeno, for example. However, the ancient way of preserving fish in salt also has a place on the menu in this region, and these simple crispy fritters are one of the many ways in which baccalà (salted cod) is used in Umbrian cooking. Try to buy fish that has already been soaked for three days to make sure that is has softened thoroughly, or you could soak it yourself, if you have the time.

1 Drain the fish, pat dry with kitchen paper and remove any bones and skin. Cut into small fillets.

2 Mix together the egg, flour and enough water to make a thick coating batter. Use the batter to cover the fish completely.

3 Heat the oil until sizzling, then fry the fish in batches until golden brown.

4 Drain the fried fish on kitchen paper to remove the excess oil, then serve the fritters piping hot.

SERVES 4

900g/2lb very fresh eels
coarse sea salt, for cleaning
150ml/¼ pint/⅔ cup extra virgin olive oil
3 garlic cloves
1 dried red chilli
3 fresh sage leaves
1 rosemary sprig
300ml/½ pint/1¼ cups white wine vinegar
sea salt

MARINATED EELS
SCAVECCIO

In the many ditches, rivers and slow-moving streams of the Tuscan plains, eels are caught and turned into delicious, simple dishes for the table. This is a very old recipe from the Pisa area, and is served cold as part of an antipasto. After 48 hours or so in the marinade, the strong, slightly muddy flavour of the eel is much reduced and the vinegar acts as a good foil to the natural oiliness of the fish.

1 Clean the outside of the eels carefully to remove all trace of slime, using coarse sea salt or gritty wood ash. Split and gut them carefully, then wash and dry them all over. Cut them into finger-length chunks.

2 Heat the oil in a frying pan and fry the eel chunks until golden brown all over. Remove them with a slotted spoon and drain on kitchen paper. Place in a bowl to cool.

3 Using the same oil, fry the garlic, chilli, sage and rosemary together for 3 minutes.

4 Add the white wine vinegar to the frying pan and then boil to reduce by about one-third. Season with salt.

5 Pour this marinade over the eels and cover the bowl. Leave to marinate for about 48 hours before serving.

PER PORTION Energy 603kcal/2499kJ; Protein 37.4g; Carbohydrate 0g, of which sugars 0g; Fat 50.4g, of which saturates 10g; Cholesterol 338mg; Calcium 43mg; Fibre 0g; Sodium 200mg.

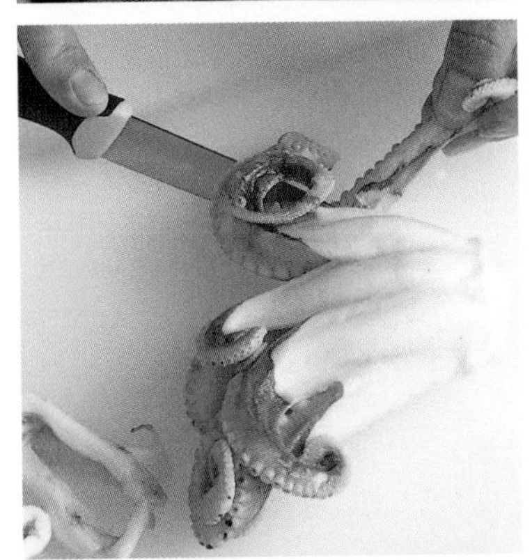

JAILED OCTOPUS
POLPO IN GALERA

The deliciously sweet taste of octopus makes it a much sought after ingredient and there are countless recipes all over Italy for this cephalopod. The name of this recipe has arisen because the octopus is traditionally cooked in a tightly sealed pot until tender and moist – the lid of the pot is never removed to stir the dish while it is cooking. It is important to use small octopuses or, if you can find them, small squid, as they are much less tough than larger specimens and will tenderize more quickly without needing to be bashed before cooking.

SERVES 6

800g/1¾lb tiny octopuses or squid
100ml/3½fl oz/scant ½ cup extra virgin olive oil
2 garlic cloves, chopped
a handful of fresh flat leaf parsley leaves, chopped
sea salt and ground black pepper

1 Clean the octopuses or squid carefully, removing eyes, beaks and bladders. Wash thoroughly in salted water. Peel the cleaned octopuses or squid and cut into small chunks.

2 Put the oil in a large pan and fry the garlic over a low heat for 5 minutes, or until soft.

3 Add the octopuses or squid. Season with salt and pepper, and cover with a lid.

4 Simmer for 30 minutes, or until tender, shaking the pan from time to time to prevent sticking. Add the fresh parsley and serve piping hot.

PER PORTION Energy 212kcal/888kJ; Protein 24.1g; Carbohydrate 0.2g, of which sugars 0.2g; Fat 12.8g, of which saturates 1.9g; Cholesterol 64mg; Calcium 61mg; Fibre 0.4g; Sodium 3mg.

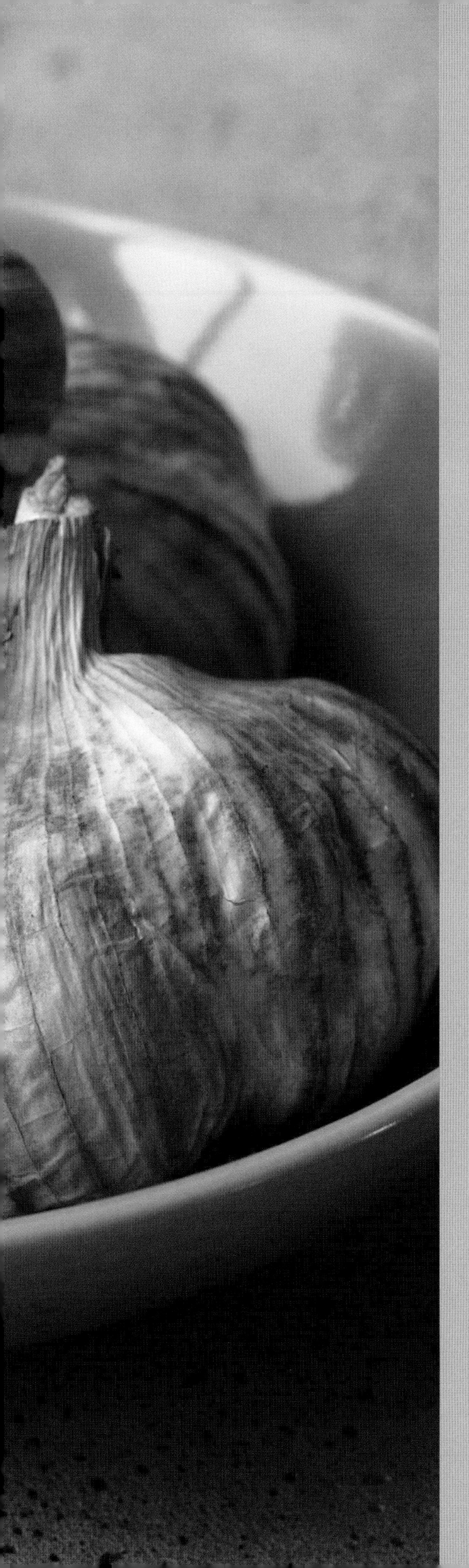

POULTRY, MEAT AND GAME

POLLAME, CARNE E CACCIA

Il secondo, or the second course, is often not considered to be as important a part of the meal as the primo for many Italians, unless of course the dish is notably special, such as in the case of game or a vast Florentine Chianina beef T-bone steak. This is not to say that there are not many preciously guarded recipes for poultry, meat and game, but for local cooks, the quality of meat and its provenance is paramount and they would much rather go without a meaty main course than use produce that does not meet their discerning standards. Prime ingredients include free-range chicken, quail, wood pigeon, guinea fowl, rabbit and wild boar, as well as succulent sausages made from the highest-quality pork, and tender beef and lamb. These are combined with fresh flavourings, such as garlic, rosemary and precious black truffle.

SLOW-COOKED GAME AND RARE GRILLED STEAK

In Tuscany, beef, veal, pork and rabbit are the most popular types of meat, alongside game such as wild boar. Beef from Chianina cattle is especially prized, and is used for the enormous, juicy T-bone steak called Bistecca alla Fiorentina, which is enough to feed at least two people. Cheaper cuts of beef are turned into stews, casseroles and pot roasts. Rabbit really comes into its own in Tuscany, where they are bred until plump and sweet for the pot and are roasted, fried or stewed in a variety of ways.

Umbrians, as well as Tuscans, love meaty, peppery pork sausages, using them in everything from pasta sauces to soups, as well as serving them as the central part of a dish. Umbrians cooks share a passion for wood pigeon, for which there are a remarkable number of recipes. Lamb is used a lot more in Umbria than in Tuscany or Le Marche.

Poultry is especially popular and most widely used in the region of Le Marche, where many recipes for chicken, guinea fowl and other birds are found, such as the delightfully quaint Guinea Fowl in a Pyramid, the delicious chicken casserole known as Drunken Chicken, or the wonderfully tangy Chicken in the Style of Macerata. Pork is also widely used in this region.

In all the regions, hunting, especially for wild boar, is part of the way of life in the countryside. The hunt is surrounded by all kinds of customs and traditions. The hunters gather together for vast feasts at the end of the season or to celebrate especially successful days. As well as being used as fresh meat, wild boar haunches are also turned into succulent cured hams. Wild truffles, which are foraged for with zeal, are used in many poultry, meat and game dishes.

CHICKEN IN THE STYLE OF MACERATA
POLLO ALLA MACERATESE

This recipe of slow-cooked chicken and livers is named after the city of Macerata, although similar versions appear on the menu in other parts of the region. Macerata is the capital of the province of the same name in Le Marche. The old centre of the city is located on a hill between the Chienti and Potenza rivers and is connected to the sprawling modern town by a lift (elevator). After two hours of cooking, the chicken is wonderfully moist, tender and full of flavour.

1 Clean and trim all the giblets and chop them coarsely. Put them in a deep pan with a lid over a medium heat and add the butter and olive oil. Cook together for 5 minutes. Lay the chicken in the pan and cook briefly on all sides to seal.

2 Pour in an even mixture of water and chicken stock to come about three-quarters of the way up the pan. Add salt and cover tightly, then simmer gently for about 1½–2 hours, or until the chicken is cooked through.

3 The liquid in the pan should have almost completely evaporated. Take the chicken out of the pan and carve it into portions. Arrange the carved chicken on a warmed serving dish.

4 Whisk together the eggs and the juice and rind of the lemon, then add to the juices left in the pan. Beat until the eggs thicken slightly.

5 Pour this sauce over the chicken portions, sprinkle with parsley and serve immediately, garnished with lemon slices.

SERVES 4 TO 6

200g/7oz chicken giblets
15g/½oz/1 tbsp unsalted butter
90ml/6 tbsp extra virgin olive oil
1 oven-ready free-range chicken, about 3kg/6lb 9oz
chicken stock, as needed
3 eggs, beaten
juice and grated rind of ½ large, unwaxed lemon
sea salt
handful chopped fresh flat leaf parsley and lemon slices, to garnish

PER PORTION Energy 765kcal/3174kJ; Protein 64.1g; Carbohydrate 0g, of which sugars 0g; Fat 56.3g, of which saturates 17.1g; Cholesterol 421mg; Calcium 40mg; Fibre 0g; Sodium 304mg.

SERVES 4 TO 6

1 oven-ready free-range chicken, about 3kg/6lb 9oz
1.75 litres/3 pints/7½ cups dry white wine, preferably Verdicchio dei Castelli di Iesi
5 garlic cloves, chopped
1 onion, sliced
1 large rosemary sprig
5 fresh sage leaves
2 celery sticks, coarsely chopped
2 carrots, coarsely chopped
a handful of fresh flat leaf parsley leaves, chopped
1 dried red chilli, chopped
10 cherry tomatoes, peeled and seeded
sea salt and ground black pepper

DRUNKEN CHICKEN
GALLINA 'MBRIACA

This recipe for chicken cooked in lots of deliciously dry and aromatic white wine comes from the region of Le Marche, where cooking and eating are always approached with joy and generosity as true pleasures of life. The wine used for this recipe would have to be the region's most famous white wine: Verdicchio dei Castelli di Iesi, which has been carefully made in the same way for decades. Verdicchio can only be produced in a specific area of Le Marche, known as Castelli di Iesi, where the terroir, climate and constant ventilation provided by the sea breezes allow the grapes to develop in a very special way. This pale, straw-coloured wine with greenish tones is delicate and flowery, with a hint of almonds and a clean, slightly bitter finish.

1 Rinse the chicken with about 600ml/1 pint/ 2½ cups of the white wine and then cover it all over, inside and out, with chopped garlic, salt and pepper. Cover and chill for at least 8 hours.

2 Joint the chicken and put it into a large bowl. Cover it completely with the remaining white wine and add the onion, rosemary, sage, celery, carrots, parsley, chilli and tomatoes.

3 Mix all the ingredients together with your hands. Cover and chill overnight.

4 The next day, transfer everything to a flameproof glazed terracotta casserole or enamel pan that has a heavy, tight-fitting lid.

5 Cover the surface of the chicken with a double sheet of baking parchment, put the lid on the top of the paper, and place a heatproof weight on the lid to press everything down as much as possible.

6 Simmer gently for about 4 hours, or until very tender, without lifting the lid. Serve.

COOK'S TIP

It is important not to move the chicken or lift the lid during the entire 4 hours of cooking.

PER PORTION Energy 862kcal/3621kJ; Protein 50.2g; Carbohydrate 74.8g, of which sugars 41.1g; Fat 24.9g, of which saturates 2.7g; Cholesterol 116mg; Calcium 151mg; Fibre 5.2g; Sodium 137mg.

SERVES 4

1 plump, oven-ready guinea fowl
1 thyme sprig
1 sage sprig
1 bay leaf
2 juniper berries, lightly crushed
4 garlic cloves, peeled and left whole
1 garlic clove, halved
900g/2lb coarse sea salt
45ml/3 tbsp plain (all-purpose) flour
1 egg white, whisked until frothy
sea salt and ground black pepper

GUINEA FOWL IN A PYRAMID
FARAONA DI PIRAMIDE

Called faraona in Italian, guinea fowl were introduced to Italy from Egypt, and in Le Marche they were considered to be a mark of distinction, enjoyed by only the aristocrats and wealthy farmers, who would serve them at wedding feasts and for other special occasions. This recipe was created by the composer Rossini's cook, for the banquet held in celebration of the première of his famous opera *Mosè in Egitto* (Moses in Egypt), which took place on 20 November 1842. The guinea fowl was theatrically unwrapped at the table when served, alongside a small hammer, which was provided to crack the hard salt crust.

1 Preheat the oven to 180°C/350°F/Gas 4. Clean and wash the guinea fowl.

2 Put the herbs, juniper berries and the peeled cloves of garlic inside the bird's cavity. Season.

3 Rub a long strip of muslin (cheesecloth) with the halved garlic clove and wrap the bird in it so that it resembles an Egyptian mummy.

4 Line the base of a high-sided ovenproof dish with 300g/11oz of the sea salt and put the wrapped guinea fowl in the centre.

5 Mix the remaining salt with the flour and, using your hands, mix in the whisked egg white to make a sticky paste.

6 Use the salt and flour paste to create a pyramid shape over the guinea fowl, covering it completely.

7 Put the guinea fowl into the preheated oven and roast for 3 hours.

8 Crack open the salt crust and take the bird out, unwrap it and carve. Serve.

COOK'S TIP

The dish was originally served with couscous shaped to look like sand dunes.

PER PORTION Energy 476kcal/1999kJ; Protein 82.5g; Carbohydrate 0g, of which sugars 0g; Fat 16.1g, of which saturates 4.1g; Cholesterol 0mg; Calcium 105mg; Fibre 0g; Sodium 225mg.

QUAIL IN THE TODI STYLE
QUAGLIA ALLA MANIERA DI TODI

This is a traditional Umbrian way of cooking quail, which works well with small pheasant or other small game birds too, particularly wood pigeon. One of the most famous hunting regions of Italy, Umbria is home to many wild animals, and game has long played a crucial role in traditional Umbrian cuisine. Todi is a very pretty town in the province of the regional capital Perugia. It sits perched on a tall, two-crested hill overlooking the east bank of the river Tiber.

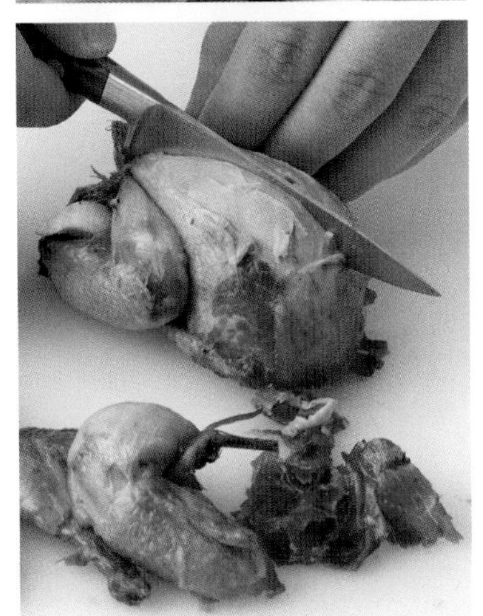

1 Preheat the oven to 180°C/350°F/Gas 4. Wrap each quail or wood pigeon in 3 sage leaves and a slice of prosciutto.

2 Put the quail into a roasting pan and roast for about 10 minutes, or until half-cooked.

3 Remove from the oven and take the meat off the carcass in large chunks, but leave the legs intact. Chop the remaining sage leaves.

4 In a pan, heat together the oil, wine, garlic, onion, pancetta, olives, capers, and remaining sage leaves for about 5 minutes.

5 Add the chunks of meat. Season with salt and pepper and cover. Leave to simmer for 1 hour, or until tender.

6 Serve the meat atop the toasted bread, with the sauce poured over.

SERVES 2

2 plump quails or wood pigeons, cleaned, rinsed, dried and ready to cook
9 fresh sage leaves
2 slices prosciutto
60ml/4 tbsp olive oil
500ml/17fl oz/2¼ cups dry red wine
2 garlic cloves, peeled and left whole
½ onion, sliced
115g/4oz pancetta, cubed
45ml/3 tbsp pitted black olives, roughly chopped
15ml/1 tbsp capers, rinsed and roughly chopped
sea salt and ground black pepper
4 slices farmhouse bread, such as ciabatta, toasted, to serve

PER PORTION Energy 631kcal/2628kJ; Protein 44.9g; Carbohydrate 1g, of which sugars 1g; Fat 31.4g, of which saturates 5.4g; Cholesterol 52mg; Calcium 54mg; Fibre 0.7g; Sodium 1671mg.

TUSCAN RABBIT CASSEROLE
CONIGLIO ALLA TOSCANA

Rabbit is a much-loved and respected meat in most parts of Italy, but perhaps especially in Tuscany, where every smallholding, farm or country home will have a few chickens and some rabbits kept for eating purposes in the back garden. Rabbit is lean and tasty, and at least 50 or so well-known recipes exist that are frequently and lovingly cooked in order to enjoy this delicious meat. This is a truly ancient recipe, apparently dating back to the time of the Etruscans, and is a thoroughly tried-and-tested way of cooking rabbit, although the method also works with jointed chicken. Serve with polenta or roast potatoes.

1 Put the rabbit joints into a bowl. Mix the wine vinegar with 600ml/1 pint/2½ cups water and pour over the rabbit. Soak for 1 hour.

2 Drain the rabbit joints and dry them carefully on kitchen paper. Chop half the garlic cloves and one rosemary sprig and mix them with the salt and pepper. Rub this mixture all over the rabbit joints.

3 Chop the remaining garlic. Heat the oil in a large pan and add the garlic and remaining rosemary. Fry the rabbit joints all over until brown. Add the red wine gradually, so that it simmers constantly.

4 Stir in the tomato purée and 300ml/½ pint/1¼ cups hot water. Cover and simmer gently for 45 minutes, or until cooked through. Serve.

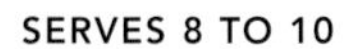

SERVES 8 TO 10

- 2 rabbits, about 900g/2lb each, each cut into five pieces
- 90ml/6 tbsp strong red or white wine vinegar
- 6 garlic cloves, peeled
- 3 large rosemary sprigs
- 2.5ml/½ tsp sea salt
- 2.5ml/½ tsp ground black pepper
- 75ml/2½fl oz/⅓ cup olive oil
- 750ml/1¼ pints/3 cups red wine
- 15ml/1 tbsp tomato purée (paste)

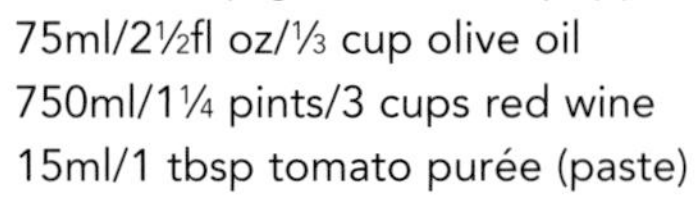

COOK'S TIP

It is possible to buy rabbit jointed and ready for the pan.

PER PORTION Energy 265kcal/1106kJ; Protein 25.2g; Carbohydrate 0.4g, of which sugars 0.4g; Fat 12.5g, of which saturates 3.7g; Cholesterol 124mg; Calcium 17mg; Fibre 0g; Sodium 40mg.

SERVES 6

45ml/3 tbsp extra virgin olive oil
2 onions, thickly sliced
2 celery sticks, thickly sliced
2 carrots, thickly sliced
900g/2lb wild boar meat
about 500ml/17fl oz/2¼ cups dry red wine
1 large rosemary sprig

FOR THE CACCIATORA SAUCE

75ml/5 tbsp extra virgin olive oil
1 garlic clove, crushed
½ large onion, chopped
1 dried red chilli
300ml/½ pint/1¼ cups Basic Tomato Sauce
sea salt

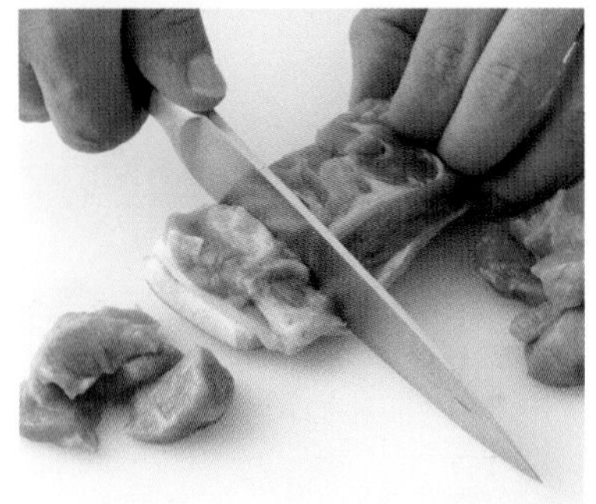

WILD BOAR CACCIATORA
CINGHIALE ALLA CACCIATORA

Cinghiale, or wild boar, is synonymous with Tuscan cuisine. In the forests and mountains of the entire region, this wild animal, closely related to the domestic pig but much stronger in flavour, has long been prized for its excellent meat. The hunting season opens in late October or early November, and the local hunters, accompanied by packs of special dogs, take great pride in seeking out these tremendously intelligent, fast-moving beasts. Serve with greens, such as spinach.

1 Put the oil in a large pan and fry the onions, celery and carrots for 10–15 minutes, or until well browned.

2 Meanwhile, cut the wild boar into large chunks and place in a deep bowl. Pour in the wine and add the rosemary and then the vegetables. The wine should cover the meat completely; add more wine if necessary and mix everything together with your hands. Leave the meat to marinate overnight.

3 Drain and dry the meat, reserving the marinade. In a wide, preferably non-stick, pan, brown all the meat so that it releases its juices.

4 Once the meat has released its liquid, remove and set it aside. Discard the liquid left in the pan.

5 To make the cacciatora sauce, add the oil to the pan with the garlic, onion and chilli. Fry together for 5 minutes, stirring, then pour over the tomato sauce. Season with salt and simmer gently for 10 minutes.

6 Add the meat to the sauce. Lower the heat, cover and simmer, stirring occasionally, for 1 hour, or until tender. Add some more of the marinade if the meat appears to be drying out while simmering. Serve with spinach, if you like.

COOK'S TIP

The cooking time for the meat will largely depend upon the age of the wild boar – the older the animal, the tougher and stringier the meat will be. For this reason, older wild boar will require much longer cooking time than young boar.

PER PORTION Energy 430kcal/1791kJ; Protein 33.8g; Carbohydrate 7.5g, of which sugars 4.7g; Fat 23.5g, of which saturates 5.1g; Cholesterol 100mg; Calcium 39mg; Fibre 1.5g; Sodium 294mg.

SERVES 4

8 plump Italian sausages
10ml/2 tsp olive oil
30ml/2 tbsp water
8 handfuls firm grapes

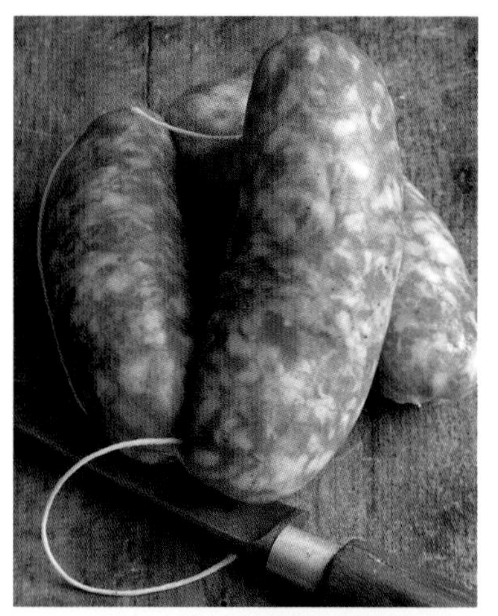

PORK SAUSAGES WITH GRAPES
SALSICCE ALL'UVA

In the early autumn, when grapes are plentiful, they make a delicious combination of flavours when fried in a pan with rich pork sausages. If the pig has been recently killed for the celebration of a local festivity, as well as to put away cured meat for the cold winter ahead, the sausages will be fresh and tender. Big, sweet, thick-skinned and firm, white grapes are best for this dish, which is like the hot-weather version of sausages with beans or lentils. However, a mixture of white and red grapes will add colour. Serve with roast potatoes and a green salad, if you like.

1 Prick the sausages all over with a knife to allow the fat to run and the heat to permeate the sausage.

2 Put the oil and water in a large frying pan over a medium heat for 2 minutes.

3 Lay the sausages in the pan. Cook gently, turning frequently, for 10 minutes, or until cooked through.

4 Add the grapes. Cook until slightly caramelized, and then serve.

PER PORTION Energy 638kcal/2648kJ; Protein 16.3g; Carbohydrate 29.7g, of which sugars 17.5g; Fat 51.3g, of which saturates 18.7g; Cholesterol 71mg; Calcium 75mg; Fibre 1.5g; Sodium 1142mg.

FLORENTINE ROAST PORK LOIN
ARISTA DI MAIALE ALLA FIORENTINA

This simple roast pork dish has a wonderful story behind it. It is an ancient Medici court recipe, from a banquet held in honour of the Greek Bishops who were journeying to Florence for the Ecumenical Council. As this was the first time the Greeks had journeyed this far, nobody was quite sure when they would arrive, so a dish had to be created that would last a few days and taste good either hot or cold. Lots of pepper, salt and garlic were used to preserve the meat as much as possible, while sweet-smelling rosemary was abundantly applied to add fragrance. When the Greeks arrived, they pronounced the meat 'Aristos!' which in ancient Greek means 'excellent', and so this tasty pork roast became known as arista for evermore.

SERVES 6

30–45ml/2–3 tbsp fresh rosemary leaves, chopped, or 25ml/1½ tbsp dried rosemary
6 large garlic cloves, finely chopped
10ml/2 tsp ground black pepper
1.3kg/3lb pork loin, boned
45–60ml/3–4 tbsp olive oil
500ml/17fl oz/2¼ cups white wine
sea salt

1 Preheat the oven to 160°C/325°F/Gas 3. Mix the rosemary with the chopped garlic. Season with salt and the black pepper.

2 Take a skewer and make lots of deep holes in the joint of meat. Insert the rosemary mixture into the holes, pushing it deep inside the flesh. Tie the joint securely with cook's string and put it into a roasting pan.

3 Rub the meat all over with oil and season with salt and pepper. Roast, basting frequently with the pan juices and with the white wine, for about 2 hours, or until cooked through. Turn the meat over each time you baste.

4 Traditionally, the joint is served cold, but is equally good hot, with the pan juices drizzled over, accompanied with peas and onions.

COOK'S TIP

Although you can use dried rosemary for convenience, fresh rosemary leaves work better for this dish, as you can achieve a softer texture once the meat is cooked.

PER PORTION Energy 369kcal/1541kJ; Protein 46.5g; Carbohydrate 0.5g, of which sugars 0.5g; Fat 14.2g, of which saturates 3.8g; Cholesterol 137mg; Calcium 23mg; Fibre 0g; Sodium 155mg.

LAMB WITH BLACK TRUFFLE
AGNELLO AL TARTUFO NERO

This rich and delicious dish of roasted lamb flavoured with mushrooms and truffle really shows off the very best of the cuisine of Umbria. This is without doubt a grand recipe of the upper-class kitchens of the region, and is a sharp contrast to the simple, basic recipes of the neighbouring peasant and shepherd communities. If fresh truffle is not available, it is always better to use a truffle butter rather than truffle oil, which is sometimes so full of chemical ingredients that it can be a long way from the real taste of precious Italian black truffle.

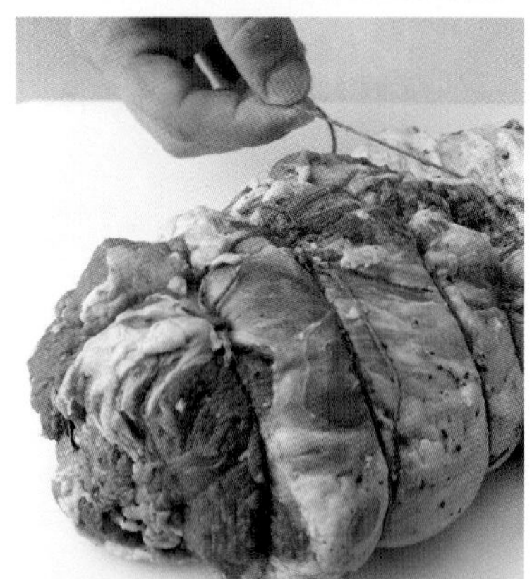

PER PORTION Energy 523kcal/2179kJ; Protein 47.2g; Carbohydrate 1.9g, of which sugars 0.2g; Fat 34g, of which saturates 10.7g; Cholesterol 213mg; Calcium 19mg; Fibre 0.9g; Sodium 171mg.

1 Preheat the oven to 180°C/350°F/Gas 4. Open out the boned leg of lamb and carefully check the meat for any bone splinters. Remove any excess fat from the lamb. (You could use the removed bone to make the lamb stock, if you like.)

2 Mix the minced meats with the truffle, kidneys, mushrooms, four of the juniper berries and 15ml/1 tbsp of the extra virgin olive oil. Season with salt and black pepper.

3 Spoon this stuffing mixture on to the inside of the opened-out lamb leg.

4 Carefully close up the lamb leg and tie it tightly and securely into shape using cook's string. Transfer it into a roasting pan. Season again on the outside with salt and black pepper, and rub it all over with the remaining olive oil.

5 Roast the lamb for about 40 minutes, turning and basting from time to time, until cooked through.

6 When it is cooked, transfer the meat to a board and leave it to rest.

7 While the meat is resting, place the roasting pan over a medium heat. Pour the red wine into the pan and boil to remove the acidity while scraping the sediment from the base of the pan.

8 Mix the stock with the potato starch or flour and stir into the roasting pan. Add the remaining juniper berries and cook, stirring, to form a reduced and thickened gravy.

9 Carve the lamb and serve with the gravy.

SERVES 8

1.8kg/4lb leg of lamb, boned
200g/7oz minced (ground) veal
200g/7oz minced (ground) pork
50g/2oz black truffle, chopped
2 lamb kidneys, trimmed and chopped
600g/1lb 6oz/8½ cups mushrooms, finely chopped
6 juniper berries, lightly crushed
45–60ml/3–4 tbsp extra virgin olive oil
250ml/8fl oz/1 cup dry red wine
about 450ml/¾ pint/scant 2 cups stock (made with the removed lamb bone, if you like)
15ml/1 tbsp potato starch or potato flour
sea salt and ground black pepper

COOK'S TIP

A dish of tender artichokes, braised with garlic and mint, is the usual accompaniment to serve alongside the lamb.

TUSCAN POT ROAST
STRACOTTO ALLA TOSCANA

This hearty pot roast is delicious served with plenty of red wine, and is often brought to the table with polenta or mashed potatoes as an accompaniment. It is cooked over an extremely low heat for about 6 hours, which gives wonderfully tender beef and a rich stock with which to make a thick and tasty sauce.

1 Pierce the meat all over with the point of a sharp knife and insert strips of garlic to taste, depending on how much you like garlic or the size of the cloves.

2 Put a large flameproof casserole over medium heat and add the pancetta, butter, onion, carrot and celery. Fry together for about 8 minutes, stirring constantly.

3 Add the meat and seal it on all sides.

4 Pour over about 300ml/½ pint/1¼ cups stock, season with salt and pepper and stir in the tomato purée.

5 Cover and simmer over a very low heat for about 6 hours, adding more stock occasionally to prevent the casserole from drying out.

6 When the meat is tender and cooked through, remove it from the casserole and set it aside to keep warm.

7 Rub the vegetables and stock left in the casserole through a sieve (strainer) or food mill, and season to taste.

8 Slice the meat thickly and arrange it on a warmed platter. Pour over the sieved sauce and serve.

SERVES 4

1.5kg/3¼lb beef brisket in a single piece
2–3 garlic cloves, cut into long strips
50g/2oz fatty pancetta, chopped
75g/3oz/6 tbsp unsalted butter
1 onion, chopped
1 carrot, chopped
1 celery stick, chopped
1 litre/1¾ pints/4 cups simmering beef stock
15ml/1 tbsp tomato purée (paste)
sea salt and ground black pepper

PER PORTION Energy 707kcal/2955kJ; Protein 81.7g; Carbohydrate 2.7g, of which sugars 2.3g; Fat 41.2g, of which saturates 20.6g; Cholesterol 254mg; Calcium 30mg; Fibre 0.7g; Sodium 537mg.

SERVES 2

3–4 rosemary sprigs
3–4 garlic cloves
30–45ml/2–3 tbsp extra virgin olive oil
1 T-bone steak, about 675g/1½lb
sea salt and ground black pepper

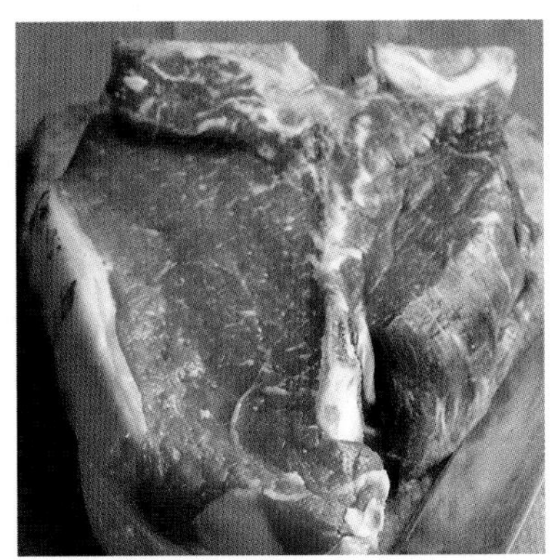

COOK'S TIP

The steak is traditionally served very rare and just seasoned to taste with salt and pepper.

PER PORTION Energy 1008kcal/4182kJ; Protein 83.1g; Carbohydrate 0.7g, of which sugars 0.6g; Fat 74.5g, of which saturates 28.3g; Cholesterol 236mg; Calcium 74mg; Fibre 1.3g; Sodium 154mg.

FLORENTINE T-BONE STEAK
BISTECCA ALLA FIORENTINA

This recipe is almost the symbol of Florentine gastronomy. A huge, luscious, rare and tender steak of Chianina beef, grilled over a scented wood fire and dressed simply with oil, rosemary, garlic, and salt and pepper (unless you are a real purist, see Cook's Tip). The fire and the wood used to cook this superb meat is actually one of the most important ingredients for the success of the dish. Many people gasp at the sight of the thickness and size of the steaks, but they are meant to be for sharing, and accompanied by just a simple salad and some good Tuscan bread. Once the steak has been washed down with a good bottle of Chianti, the beauty of this very Tuscan eating experience becomes apparent.

1 Bruise the rosemary and garlic by bashing them lightly with a rolling pin.

2 Place the bruised rosemary and garlic in a flat dish, then add the olive oil. Stir to mix, then add the steak and leave to marinate for 24–48 hours.

3 Light the barbecue and, when the flames have died down, position the grill rack over the hot coals. Cook the steak to taste. Alternatively, preheat a grill (broiler) to high, then cook the steak for 2 minutes on each side for medium-rare, or 3–4 minutes for well-done.

VEGETABLES, EGGS AND CHEESE

VERDURE, UOVA E FORMAGGIO

Beautifully fresh, seasonal vegetables are a fundamental part of life when it comes to cooking and eating in any part of Italy, and the regions of Tuscany, Umbria and Le Marche are no exception. The basic philosophy which lies at the root of all authentic Italian cooking is that the ingredients should be as fresh as possible, locally available and used only when in season. Wild vegetables such as mushrooms and asparagus are especially cherished. Eggs have always been a staple food, but when they are combined with delicious vegetables and a little local cheese, they are transformed into the most wonderful flat omelettes, or frittatas, which make a fabulous filling for sandwiches. They can also be served as a substitute for meat or fish, with some crisp salad or a bowlful of sliced ruby red tomatoes drizzled with extra virgin olive oil.

PECORINO, TRUFFLES AND HERBY FRITTATAS

The thrill of expectation for each vegetable or fruit coming into its season throughout the year is one of those small, simple pleasures that most Italian children grow up appreciating. Each new vegetable arrives on the market stalls with a flutter of excitement and anticipation, to be immediately and eagerly made the most of while the season lasts. The Italian word 'primizie' is used to describe the tiny new vegetables, such as tender salads and sweet baby peas, which make their first tentative appearance after the winter is over. They really are the first definite signs of spring.

The tradition of foraging is alive and well. All over these regions, roadside grass verges, fields, woods and forests are considered perfect places to find delicious wild vegetables. From mushrooms, salad leaves and herbs to wild asparagus and precious truffles, natural ingredients are carefully sought out, picked and taken home to the kitchen. The wonderful mixture of wild salad leaves gathered from the countryside is known in Italy as 'misticanza'.

Tuscany produces many of Italy's most prized Pecorino cheeses, especially around the town of Pienza. This ewe's milk cheese has a slightly sharper flavour than cow's milk cheese. Markets in Pienza display rows of Pecorino in varying stages of maturity, many flavoured with chillis, truffles, wines or herbs. Ricotta, a by-product of the hard cheese, is used in many local dishes. As it has such a bland, creamy flavour, ricotta is very useful for both savoury and sweet dishes.

Eggs are treated with the same respect that is afforded to other ingredients. Italian cooks who live in the country will usually keep a few chickens for the pot as well as for their free-range eggs.

FRITTATA WITH FRESH HERBS
FRITTATA CON LE ERBETTE ODOROSE

A frittata, made with all the wild herbs one can possibly find, is typical of the Easter period, when the first spring shoots are plentiful. Everything goes into the mixture, such as wild asparagus or cultivated thin asparagus, wild garlic leaves, wild hops, borage, chicory and many more. These are combined with whatever is available in the vegetable garden, such as pea shoots, broad bean shoots, broccoli or rocket (arugula) flowers, the new season's tiny artichokes, and so on; there is no limit to the possible combinations. This is a typical recipe from Umbria, where wild edible plants are widely available all over the countryside in the springtime. Serve the frittata either hot or cold with salad, if you like.

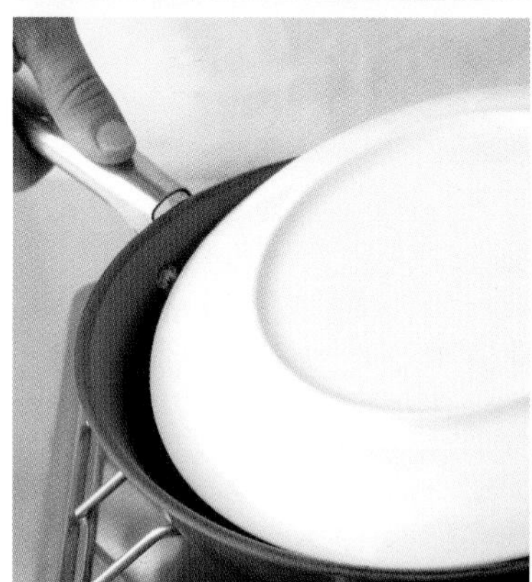

1 Put the oil in a non-stick frying pan and add 45ml/3 tbsp cold water. Add the garlic, spring onions, mint, lemon balm, flat leaf parsley and chervil, and cook for 5 minutes, or until softened.

2 Beat the eggs together in a small bowl, then season them with salt and pepper.

3 Pour the beaten eggs into the frying pan with the herb mixture and stir gently with a wooden spoon to combine.

4 As the egg begins to set, rock the pan slightly from side to side and pull the outer edge of the frittata towards the centre, making sure the underneath of the frittata sets completely, without burning.

5 Cover the frittata with a plate that is larger than the pan. Turn it over in one smooth movement, so that it lands safely on the plate.

6 If the pan looks completely dry, add a little more oil, then slide the frittata back into the hot pan, starting at the opposite side of the pan and drawing the plate back towards you.

7 Shake the frittata into position, flatten gently with a spatula, and cook until golden brown underneath.

8 Slide the frittata out on to a platter and serve hot or cold, cut into wedges, with a green salad, if you like.

SERVES 4

about 45ml/3 tbsp extra virgin olive oil
1 garlic bulb, cloves chopped
5 small spring onions (scallions), chopped
a small bunch of fresh mint leaves, chopped
a small handful of fresh lemon balm leaves, chopped
a small handful of fresh flat leaf parsley leaves, chopped
a small handful of fresh chervil leaves, chopped
8 eggs
sea salt and ground black pepper
salad leaves, to serve (optional)

VARIATION

Vary the herbs according to what you have available.

PER PORTION Energy 235kcal/975kJ; Protein 13.7g; Carbohydrate 1.7g, of which sugars 0.4g; Fat 19.6g, of which saturates 4.3g; Cholesterol 381mg; Calcium 115mg; Fibre 0.2g; Sodium 145mg.

BLACK TRUFFLE FRITTATA
FRITTATA AL TARTUFO

This recipe is made using the black truffle of Umbria, which is liberally used in many dishes throughout the region. These elusive fungi grow under the trees in the local woods and forests and are sought out by specially trained dogs, then dug up by the truffle hunters. Although neither as expensive nor as intensely flavoured as the white Piedmontese truffle of Alba, black truffles taste unique, and are highly prized both within the region and throughout the world. The international black truffle festival of Umbria always takes place over the last weekend of February in the lovely medieval town of Spoleto. The flavours of truffles and eggs marry together beautifully, so this frittata has a taste that is really very special.

SERVES 4

9 eggs
115g/4oz sliced fresh black truffles or sliced truffles preserved in oil (tartufata)
about 45ml/3 tbsp extra virgin olive oil
45ml/3 tbsp dry white wine
sea salt and ground black pepper

COOK'S TIP

If using a fresh truffle, you'll need to brush it clean with a special little brush, or a brand-new nailbrush. Never wash them! To slice, use a special truffle slicer or a mandolin to get the slices extremely thin.

1 Beat the eggs together in a small bowl, then season them with salt and pepper.

2 Mix the sliced truffles into the beaten egg mixture.

3 Heat the oil in a large frying pan and swirl it around to coat it thoroughly. Pour the egg and truffle mixture into the frying pan.

4 As the egg begins to set, carefully rock the pan slightly from side to side and pull the outer edge of the frittata towards the centre, making sure the underneath of the frittata sets completely, without burning.

5 Cover the frittata with a plate that is larger than the pan. Turn the frittata over in one smooth movement, so that it lands safely on the plate.

6 If the pan looks completely dry, add a little more olive oil, then slide the frittata back into the hot pan, starting at the opposite side of the pan and drawing the plate back towards you.

7 Shake the frittata into position, flatten gently with a spatula, and cook until golden brown underneath.

8 Sprinkle with the wine, slide out on to a platter and serve immediately, piping hot.

PER PORTION Energy 251kcal/1040kJ; Protein 14.6g; Carbohydrate 0.2g, of which sugars 0.1g; Fat 20.9g, of which saturates 4.7g; Cholesterol 428mg; Calcium 67mg; Fibre 0.3g; Sodium 160mg.

THE FLAG
LA BANDIERA

This Umbrian pepper stew is almost a purée by the time it has been cooked gently for almost 40 minutes, but it is really delicious either as a side dish with meat or as part of an antipasto. It can even be added to beaten eggs and turned into the most flavoursome frittata, and is also good with cheese. The name of the dish is thought to refer to the brightness of the colour: bright and strident like a red flag.

1 First, peel the tomatoes. Place the tomatoes in a large heatproof bowl and cover with boiling water. Leave for 30 seconds, then carefully drain them. The skins should peel off easily. Chop the flesh, discarding the seeds.

2 Put the oil in a pan and fry the onion for 5 minutes, or until softened but not browned.

3 Add the sliced peppers, stir, and cook for 10 minutes.

4 Add the chopped tomatoes, season with salt and stir well. Simmer the mixture gently, stirring frequently, for about 30 minutes, or until the peppers and tomatoes have softened completely.

SERVES 4

450g/1lb ripe tomatoes
45ml/3 tbsp extra virgin olive oil
1 onion, sliced
450g/1lb red (bell) peppers, seeded and sliced
sea salt

PER PORTION Energy 129kcal/538kJ; Protein 1.9g; Carbohydrate 10.7g, of which sugars 10.4g; Fat 9g, of which saturates 1.4g; Cholesterol 0mg; Calcium 17mg; Fibre 2.9g; Sodium 15mg.

SERVES 4

1.2kg/2½lb fresh peas in their pods, or 450g/1lb shelled peas
100ml/3½fl oz/scant ½ cup olive oil
1 onion, thinly sliced
2.5ml/½ tsp caster (superfine) sugar
sea salt and ground black pepper

VARIATION

Fry a little chopped pancetta or fatty prosciutto crudo with the onion, if you like.

COOK'S TIP

Use a cast-iron pan for this dish if you have one.

PER PORTION Energy 280kcal/1157kJ; Protein 9g; Carbohydrate 21.3g, of which sugars 8.9g; Fat 18.4g, of which saturates 2.7g; Cholesterol 0mg; Calcium 49mg; Fibre 6.7g; Sodium 4mg.

PEAS COOKED IN OLIVE OIL
PISELLI ALL'OLIO

Peas cooked in this way can be added to a delicious frittata, or mixed with a little warmed cream to dress pasta, with just a sprinkling of freshly grated Parmesan cheese and black pepper to finish it off. The peas are soaked first, which means that they soften without cooking, and their natural sweetness develops perfectly.

1 Soak the peas in cold water for 1 hour.

2 Meanwhile, put the olive oil in a flameproof casserole or heavy pan and add the sliced onion. Fry the onion over a low heat for about 10 minutes, or until it has softened and turned golden brown in colour.

3 Drain the peas and add to the onion. Add the sugar, season with salt and pepper, then cover and cook gently until soft and cooked through. The timing will depend on how large or small the peas are: tiny ones will take about 4 minutes; larger, fat peas with tougher skins could take up to 15 minutes.

STEWED BEANS
FAGIOLI ALL'UCCELLETTO

Tuscans love their beans, and this recipe is a real classic, one you will find all year round all over the region, but especially in and around Florence. Delicious hot or cold, this recipe can be served on its own or as part of another dish, for example on top of toasted bread as crostini or alongside meat or fish dishes. It is a very adaptable bean dish that can be made with canned or dried beans, or fresh beans when they are in season. If using dried beans, soak them overnight in cold water, boil hard in fresh water for 5 minutes, then rinse and use as fresh. Sometimes it is made with rosemary instead of sage, though the sage gives a more subtle flavour.

SERVES 4

45–60ml/3–4 tbsp olive oil
3 cloves garlic, peeled and crushed
2 or 3 leaves fresh sage
400g/14oz can cannellini beans, drained
200g/7oz canned tomatoes, strained
sea salt and ground black pepper

1 Put the oil in a pan and gently fry the garlic and sage.

2 When the oil is golden brown, add the beans and season with a pinch of ground black pepper.

3 Stir the mixture together thoroughly, then add the strained tomatoes. Simmer gently for a further 20 minutes.

4 Check and adjust the seasoning to taste, then serve.

PER PORTION Energy 160kcal/669kJ; Protein 6.3g; Carbohydrate 14.6g, of which sugars 2.7g; Fat 8.9g, of which saturates 1.3g; Cholesterol 0mg; Calcium 19mg; Fibre 5.1g; Sodium 425mg.

GREEN BEANS IN THE FLORENTINE STYLE
FAGIOLINI ALLA FIORENTINA

This is a sure-fire way to liven up green beans. Even frozen green beans, which are rarely tasty, take on a new lease of life with this very simple Florentine recipe. For this dish, Florentine cooks use the dried fennel seed that is so popular in local recipes and in many culinary specialities, including the huge soft salame known locally as finocchiona, which is so soft that it is almost spreadable, and has a strong fennel flavour. Like so many of these kinds of stewed vegetable dishes that are popular all over Italy, the beans are allowed to cook until they are really soft and have absorbed as much as possible of the surrounding flavours.

SERVES 4

7.5ml/1½ tsp fennel seeds
450g/1lb green beans, trimmed
75ml/5 tbsp olive oil
1 large red onion, thinly sliced
20ml/4 tsp tomato purée (paste) diluted in 60ml/4 tbsp hot water
sea salt and ground black pepper

PER PORTION Energy 181kcal/747kJ; Protein 3.3g; Carbohydrate 10.2g, of which sugars 7.4g; Fat 14.5g, of which saturates 2.1g; Cholesterol 0mg; Calcium 62mg; Fibre 3.7g; Sodium 14mg.

1 Crush the fennel seeds to a powder in a spice grinder or using a mortar and pestle.

2 Boil the beans in a pan of lightly salted water until tender.

3 Meanwhile, heat the oil in a large frying pan, add the onion and fry until soft.

4 Stir in the diluted tomato purée and the crushed fennel seeds.

5 Drain the beans thoroughly and toss them into the pan. Mix well and season to taste.

6 Cover and cook through for 10–15 minutes more, then serve.

DEEP-FRIED COURGETTES
ZUCCHINI FRITTI

This is a recipe from Tuscany, although other versions of the same dish exist more or less all over the country. It can be made with courgette flowers, if they are available, but using thin slices of courgette is much simpler and tastes delicious. If you do choose to use flowers, check them on the inside for insects before proceeding, and remove the pistil, which will taste bitter.

SERVES 4

2 courgettes (zucchini)
1 egg, separated
40g/1½oz/⅓ cup plain (all-purpose) flour
150ml/¼ pint/⅔ cup milk, or milk mixed with water
600ml/1 pint/2½ cups sunflower oil
sea salt

1 Cut the courgettes into thin strips with a potato peeler or mandolin.

2 In a bowl, beat together the egg yolk, flour and milk, or mixed milk and water, to make a smooth paste. Put the egg white into a clean, grease-free bowl and whisk until stiff. Gently fold into the batter.

3 Carefully dip the courgettes into the batter to coat thoroughly.

4 Heat the oil in a wide, deep pan until a small cube of bread dropped into it sizzles instantly.

5 Carefully lower the courgette strips into the hot oil and deep-fry for 4 minutes, or until crisp and golden all over, turning frequently. (If they take longer than this the oil is not hot enough.)

6 Drain thoroughly on kitchen paper, sprinkle with a little salt and serve immediately.

VARIATIONS

If using courgette flowers, you could try filling them before frying:
- For a punchy flavour, push a small piece of anchovy and a cube of mozzarella cheese into the centre of the flower.
- For a smooth, sweet taste that contrasts brilliantly with the crispy fried flower, use a spoonful of ricotta cheese.

PER PORTION Energy 187kcal/774kJ; Protein 5.4g; Carbohydrate 11.5g, of which sugars 3.7g; Fat 13.5g, of which saturates 2.2g; Cholesterol 53mg; Calcium 90mg; Fibre 1.2g; Sodium 40mg.

SERVES 6

- 200g/7oz ready-to-cook spelt
- 4 potatoes, quartered
- 4 courgettes (zucchini), halved
- 115g/4oz green beans
- 200g/7oz fresh haricot (navy) or cannellini beans
- 275g/10oz cabbage leaves, shredded
- 3 carrots (or similar quantity of other vegetables of your choice)
- 115g/4oz thinly sliced pancetta
- 3 garlic cloves, peeled and left whole
- 15ml/1 tbsp extra virgin olive oil
- 1 dried red chilli, chopped
- sea salt

SPELT WITH VEGETABLES
FARRO E VERDURA

Spelt is a species of wheat grain. It was an important staple food in various parts of Europe from the Bronze Age to medieval times, but has survived as part of the daily diet in various parts of Italy, including Tuscany, Umbria and Le Marche. More recently, it has found a new market as a health food and as a substitute for common wheat for those with a gluten intolerance or allergy. Nutty and delicious, spelt is used in soups, salads or casseroles, or is ground to a flour for bread and pasta making. This recipe is from Le Marche.

1 Boil the spelt in plenty of lightly salted water for 50 minutes–1 hour, until tender.

2 Meanwhile, boil the potatoes in a separate pan for 10 minutes, then add the courgettes, green beans, haricot beans, cabbage leaves and carrots and cook for a further 10–15 minutes, until tender. Drain both the cooked spelt and the cooked vegetables.

3 In a large frying pan, fry the pancetta and garlic in the oil until the garlic is softened and the pancetta is crispy. Discard the garlic.

4 Add the spelt and all the vegetables to the frying pan. Mix well and season with salt and the dried red chilli.

5 Fry for 5 minutes to heat through, then serve.

COOK'S TIP

Serve as an accompaniment to boiled or grilled (broiled) meats, or with a thick slice of crusty bread, rubbed with a garlic clove and drizzled with extra virgin olive oil.

PER PORTION Energy 305kcal/1288kJ; Protein 11.6g; Carbohydrate 50g, of which sugars 5.6g; Fat 7.9g, of which saturates 2.1g; Cholesterol 12mg; Calcium 68mg; Fibre 4.5g; Sodium 396mg.

SERVES 4

1 large spring cabbage
300ml/½ pint/1¼ cups extra virgin olive oil
100ml/3½fl oz/scant ½ cup red wine vinegar
3 garlic cloves, lightly crushed
sea salt and ground black pepper

WARM SPRING CABBAGE SALAD
CAVOLINA IN INSALATA

A very simple recipe for a warm cabbage salad from Le Marche, this dish is perfect served alongside the many pork or chicken dishes from this region. The recipe does call for fresh, crisp, spring cabbage as opposed to the coarser, heavier-leaved cabbages such as Savoy or the Tuscan cavolo nero. As with all recipes that rely on very few, basic ingredients, it is important that the flavourings, in this case the red wine vinegar, should be of the best possible quality – in other words, strong and tasty as well as sharp and sour, but not too astringent or acidic.

1 Remove the hard outer leaves of the cabbage. Shred the rest of the cabbage finely and put it into a colander. Rinse it well several times, then drain thoroughly.

2 Pour the oil and vinegar into a pan over a medium heat. Add the garlic. Heat until sizzling.

3 Transfer the shredded cabbage to a salad bowl, then pour over the hot garlic oil. Toss the mixture together thoroughly.

4 Season with salt and pepper, toss again and cover with a plate to allow it to steam for about 2–3 minutes. Serve.

COOK'S TIP

You could save the hard outer leaves of the cabbage to add to other vegetables for vegetable stock, or use them for a soup such as minestrone.

PER PORTION Energy 484kcal/1991kJ; Protein 1.9g; Carbohydrate 6.2g, of which sugars 5.6g; Fat 50.2g, of which saturates 7g; Cholesterol 0mg; Calcium 56mg; Fibre 2.5g; Sodium 8mg.

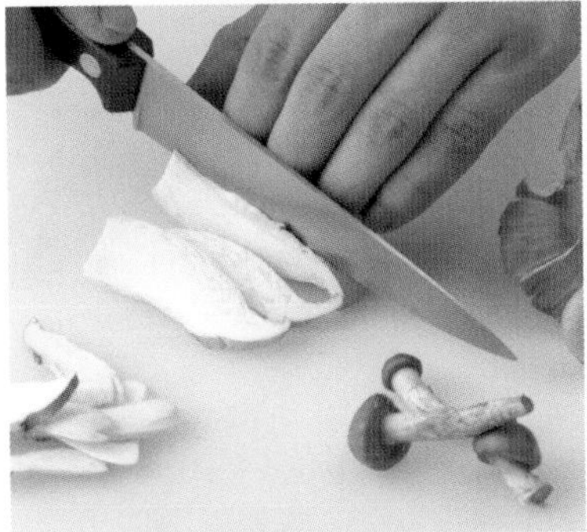

WILD MUSHROOM SALAD
INSALATA DI FUNGHI CRUDI

This delicately flavoured salad makes the most of the special taste of raw mushrooms, and is traditionally made using fresh porcini or other wild mushrooms. If picking wild mushrooms to make this salad, you must make sure that the mushrooms are edible, and also that they are safe to eat raw as some varieties do require cooking. You can also make the salad using cultivated mushrooms or field mushrooms, but the important thing to remember is that they need to be sliced as thinly as possible. The salad should be eaten soon after preparation, within half an hour at the most, so that the mushrooms don't shrivel up.

SERVES 4

500g/1¼lb mixed wild or cultivated mushrooms
200g/7oz Parmesan cheese
a large handful of fresh flat leaf parsley leaves, finely chopped
juice of ½ lemon
extra virgin olive oil, to drizzle
sea salt and ground black pepper

1 Clean and trim the mushrooms carefully. Do not wash them, but use a brush to clean off any traces of soil.

2 Once clean, slice the mushrooms very thinly. Shave the Parmesan as thinly as possible.

3 Arrange the sliced mushrooms on a large platter, then sprinkle the chopped parsley and Parmesan shavings over the top.

4 Sprinkle with lemon juice, drizzle with oil and season. Serve within half an hour.

COOK'S TIP

Choose a mildly flavoured olive oil for drizzling over this salad, so that you do not overpower the mushrooms.

PER PORTION Energy 247kcal/1027kJ; Protein 22.3g; Carbohydrate 0.9g, of which sugars 0.5g; Fat 17.2g, of which saturates 10.4g; Cholesterol 50mg; Calcium 633mg; Fibre 2g; Sodium 556mg.

DESSERTS AND BAKING DOLCI

The tradition of desserts and cakes in these regions is generally quite simple: they contain lots of spices, nuts, such as almonds and walnuts, and fresh, dried and candied fruit. The reason for this dates back to medieval times when many of the cities in this area were gateways for carriages and wagons travelling from the Orient. Consequently, a large number of dessert recipes have evolved over time with a unique Eastern edge to them, using a whole host of exotic spices, as well as locally produced honey, nuts and dried fruits. The prevalence of these ingredients means that Tuscany, Umbria and Le Marche share similar recipes. Throughout Italy, fruitcakes are mainly eaten during the Christmas festive season but in Central Italy they are eaten all year round. For this reason, towns such as Siena, which are famous throughout Italy for their age-old baking tradition, always have the distinctive perfume of cakes and spices lingering in the air.

ALMONDS, HONEY AND CANDIED FRUITS

There are two main types of sweet cake found in Central Italy: Panforte and Panpepato. Both cakes originate from the medieval recipe for focaccia alla frutta. Many of the local cakes and desserts have been adapted from these two cakes over the centuries.

Panforte has the rich flavours of honey, nuts, dried fruits and Eastern spices. When baked, the cake mixture should be left slightly damp so that the cake retains a distinctive sharp, bitter taste for which it is named: in this context, the word 'forte' actually means bitter. The first official Panforte was introduced at Siena's famous annual horse racing tournament, the Palio, in 1879 in the hope of impressing the royal family. The local chefs thought that the original recipe was not suitable for royalty, so they created a completely new product in honour of the Queen, thus naming it Panforte Margherita.

As far as Panpepato goes, legend has it that when the city of Siena was under siege, a nun called Sister Berta, concerned for the health of the local residents, decided to make a cake for the hard-working men in order to give them strength. She used the traditional recipe for focaccia alla frutta, replacing the fresh fruit with candied fruit, and adding large quantities of almonds, ginger, pepper and other sweet spices. Sister Berta succeeded in boosting the health of the people and Panpepato is now considered a cake that unites a family. It is less sweet and slightly more spicy than Panforte.

Other local biscuits, cakes and desserts that share these flavours include Soft Almond Sweetmeats (ricciarelli), the famous Tuscan Hard Dunking Cookies (cantucci), and the less well-known but ancient Tuscan Honey Cookies (cavallucci).

TUSCAN CREAM AND CHOCOLATE PUDDING
ZUCCOTTO

This delicious iced pudding is intended to look like the traditional helmet of a Tuscan mercenary going into battle, which in turn was named after a small, rounded pumpkin. It's not difficult to make; the most fiddly part is the stencilling at the end. If you prefer, just dust the whole thing with icing sugar and then lightly dust over the top with cocoa powder. This is a great dessert to keep as a standby in the freezer. Divide the mixture in half and make two smaller bowls if you wish.

SERVES 6 TO 8

75g/3oz/½ cup hazelnuts
115g/4oz unsweetened cooking chocolate
ready-made basic sponge cake, preferably 25cm/10in
90ml/6 tbsp brandy
60ml/4 tbsp amaretto liqueur
1 litre/1¾ pints/4 cups double (heavy) cream
75g/3oz/½ cup blanched almonds, coarsely chopped
30ml/2 tbsp plain (semisweet) chocolate drops
30ml/2 tbsp chopped mixed crystallized (candied) peel or glacé (candied) fruits
150g/5oz/1¼ cups icing (confectioners') sugar, sifted, plus extra for dusting
30ml/2 tbsp unsweetened cocoa powder, for dusting

1 Lay the hazelnuts out on a baking sheet and toast them under a hot grill (broiler), turning occasionally, for about 5 minutes, or until golden.

2 Hold a few hazelnuts at a time in a dish towel and rub off their skins. Cool and chop, then set aside.

3 Melt the chocolate in a heatproof bowl over a pan of gently simmering water. Remove the bowl from the pan.

4 Take a large bowl (large enough to take all the cake and the cream) and draw a circle slightly larger than the bowl's circumference on a sheet of stiff paper. Cut out the circle and set it aside. Line the bowl with foil.

5 Slice the cake into strips about 4cm/1½in wide, dip each strip in brandy, then in amaretto, and press the strips against the sides of the bowl to line it. Set aside.

6 In a large bowl, whip the cream until stiff peaks form. Fold the hazelnuts, almonds, chocolate drops, crystallized peel or glacé fruits, and sugar into the cream.

7 Transfer half the cream mixture to another bowl. Stir the melted chocolate into one half of the cream.

8 Spoon the white cream over the base and sides of the cake-lined bowl, then use the chocolate cream to fill the hollow in the centre. Level the top with a spatula. Place the bowl in the freezer for at least 3 hours.

9 Meanwhile, fold the circle of paper into eight and cut out four alternate sections.

10 Shortly before serving, turn the zuccotto out on to a platter. Remove the foil carefully, and, using a sieve (strainer), dust with the remaining icing sugar.

11 Lay the cut-out circle of paper on top of the zuccotto. Carefully hold it in place and dust it with the cocoa powder. Remove the paper carefully. You should now have alternate segments of brown and white, which is the traditional design. Serve immediately.

COOK'S TIP

This dessert contains alcohol, so is not suitable for children.

PER PORTION Energy 1087kcal/4507kJ; Protein 9.9g; Carbohydrate 56.5g, of which sugars 44.8g; Fat 96.3g, of which saturates 45.5g; Cholesterol 233mg; Calcium 147mg; Fibre 2.2g; Sodium 245mg.

PASTA WITH SWEET WALNUT SAUCE
NOCIATA

Most people do not associate pasta with desserts, but this unusual recipe is very much a part of the Umbrian culinary tradition, and the texture of pasta works perfectly with the sweet, nutty sauce. It was created to be a part of the Vigilia (Christmas Eve) feast, in times when this special festive meal had a formal, ceremonial atmosphere. All over Italy, the main Christmas meal takes place on Christmas Eve, either after midnight mass or before the mass, depending on the regional custom. It is usually served cold.

SERVES 4

300g/11oz/2¾ cups short pasta, such as penne, tortiglione or maccheroni
150g/5oz/scant 1 cup walnuts, broken
50g/2oz/¼ cup sugar
grated rind of 1 large unwaxed lemon
5ml/1 tsp ground cinnamon
5ml/1 tsp unsweetened cocoa powder (optional)
25g/1oz/2 tbsp unsalted butter
pinch of sea salt

1 Bring 3 litres/5¼ pints/12½ cups salted water to the boil in a large pan. Add the pasta, cover and return to the boil. Cook according to the pack instructions until just tender; do not overcook.

2 Put the walnuts into a food processor. Using the blade attachment, process to a fine mass with the sugar, lemon rind, cinnamon and cocoa, if using. Reserve a little lemon rind to garnish. (Alternatively, pound the walnuts in a mortar and pestle, and stir in the sugar, lemon rind, cinnamon and cocoa.)

3 Transfer the walnut mixture to a large serving dish. Remove a ladleful of the boiling water from the pasta and stir into the walnut mixture.

4 Drain the pasta and add to the walnut mixture. Add the butter, then toss all the ingredients together well to distribute the sauce evenly.

5 Leave to stand for 5 minutes, then serve, sprinkled with the reserved lemon rind. Alternatively, leave to cool and serve cold.

PER PORTION Energy 618kcal/2588kJ; Protein 15.1g; Carbohydrate 70.2g, of which sugars 16.5g; Fat 32.7g, of which saturates 6g; Cholesterol 14mg; Calcium 65mg; Fibre 3.8g; Sodium 76mg.

SOFT ALMOND SWEETMEATS
I RICCIARELLI

These delicately flavoured Tuscan soft almond sweetmeats can be bought in all good Italian food stores and are traditionally eaten at Christmas time. The bought versions are perfectly shaped, like large lozenges, and pure white in colour. This recipe for home-made ricciarelli gives you a slightly less aesthetically faultless result, but is delicious nonetheless and perfect with a glass of chilled, sweet, amber-coloured Vinsanto. It is customary to bake these on a host – a small piece of edible paper that forms the base and is eaten with the sweetmeat – but they can also be cooked directly on a sheet of baking parchment.

MAKES ABOUT 12

200g/7oz/generous 1 cup blanched almonds
115g/4oz/⅔ cup pine nuts
200g/7oz/1 cup caster (superfine) sugar
5ml/1 tsp vanilla extract
2 egg whites
grated rind of ½ small unwaxed orange
115g/4oz/1 cup icing (confectioners') sugar, sifted

1 Pound the blanched almonds and the pine nuts together to make a fine powder using a mortar and pestle, or alternatively, pulse in a food processor.

2 Transfer into a bowl and add the caster sugar and vanilla extract. Mix thoroughly.

3 Put the egg whites into a clean, grease-free bowl and whisk into stiff peaks – you should be able to turn the bowl upside down and the egg whites remain inside.

4 Carefully fold the grated orange rind into the egg whites, then fold in the almond mixture.

5 Line a baking sheet with baking parchment, then put heaped tablespoonfuls of the mixture on to the parchment, set well apart. Chill for about 6 hours.

6 Preheat the oven to 150°C/300°F/Gas 2. Bake the sweetmeats for 15 minutes. Cool on a wire rack and sprinkle generously with the icing sugar before serving.

PER PORTION Energy 273kcal/1144kJ; Protein 5.5g; Carbohydrate 29g, of which sugars 28.5g; Fat 15.9g, of which saturates 1.2g; Cholesterol 0mg; Calcium 55mg; Fibre 1.4g; Sodium 14mg.

TUSCAN HONEY COOKIES
I CAVALLUCCI

The Italian name of these little cookies literally translates as 'little horses', as they were once made for the riders and stablehands of the famous horse race, known as Palio, which is run in Siena twice a year. Over the years, the cookies gradually became so popular that they are now almost as well known, and certainly as typical, as the famous panforte di Siena, the hard, spicy, fruit-laden flat cake that originates from the town. These cookies are wonderfully chewy and strongly flavoured with aniseed, and are traditionally eaten around Christmas time.

SERVES 8

115g/4oz/⅔ cup almonds
200g/7oz/1 cup caster (superfine) sugar
115g/4oz/½ cup acacia honey
450g/1lb/4 cups plain (all-purpose) flour, plus extra for dusting
115g/4oz/½ cup crystallized (candied) citrus fruits, finely chopped
30ml/2 tbsp fennel seeds
a pinch each of ground cinnamon, freshly grated nutmeg and ground coriander
1.5ml/¼ tsp bicarbonate of soda (baking soda), or ammonium carbonate, if available
oil, for greasing

1 Blanch the almonds by soaking them in hot water for about 1 minute, then removing the skins. Alternatively, use ready-blanched almonds.

2 Lay the almonds out on a baking sheet and toast them under a hot grill (broiler), turning occasionally, for about 5 minutes, or until golden. Keep checking the almonds regularly as they burn easily. Chop the almonds coarsely.

3 Put the sugar and honey into a large, heavy pan and melt together very slowly over a low heat.

4 When the mixture is hot enough to form a string as you lift up the spoon, very gradually mix in the flour, then the crystallized citrus fruits, fennel seeds, blanched almonds and spices. Then stir in the bicarbonate of soda or ammonium carbonate.

5 Flour the work surface well, then spread the mixture out on the floured surface to a thickness of about 1cm/½in, using a spatula dipped in water to help you spread it easily. Leave the cookie mixture to cool completely on the floured work surface. Preheat the oven to 180°C/350°F/Gas 4.

6 Cut into rectangles and lay them carefully on a well-oiled baking sheet.

7 Bake the cookies for 20 minutes, or until golden.

8 Remove from the oven, then cool the cookies on a wire rack. Store them in an airtight container for up to 1 week.

VARIATION

Although it is traditional to use acacia honey in this recipe, you could use another variety.

PER PORTION Energy 461kcal/1950kJ; Protein 8.9g; Carbohydrate 91.3g, of which sugars 47.2g; Fat 9.2g, of which saturates 0.8g; Cholesterol 0mg; Calcium 150mg; Fibre 3.5g; Sodium 48mg.

SERVES 8 TO 10

oil, for greasing
225g/8oz/1⅓ cups almonds
1kg/2¼lb plain (all-purpose) flour, sifted
8 eggs, beaten
1kg/2¼lb/generous 5 cups caster (superfine) sugar
10ml/2 tsp ammonium carbonate (see Cook's Tip)
pinch of salt

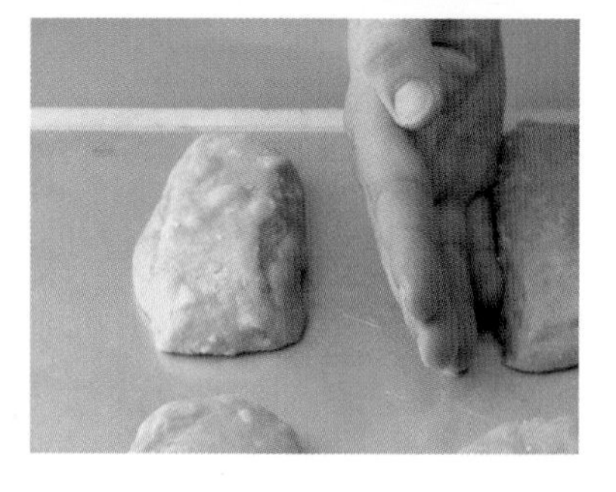

TUSCAN HARD DUNKING COOKIES
CANTUCCI

Italians love to dunk, and these cookies are made for being dunked into a glass of Vinsanto, Tuscany's favourite sweet dessert wine, or a cup of dark and fragrant espresso coffee, to make a simple but very satisfying dessert. Recently, these tasty little cookies have become hugely popular all over the world and a host of recipes exist for them, using all kinds of weird and wonderful ingredients, from pink peppercorns to hazelnut liqueur. This is the classic, much-loved recipe from their native Tuscany.

1 Preheat the oven to 150°C/300°F/Gas 2. Oil two baking sheets. Blanch the almonds by soaking them in hot water for about 1 minute, then removing the skins.

2 Lay the almonds out on a baking sheet and toast them under a hot grill (broiler), turning occasionally, for about 5 minutes, or until golden. Chop coarsely.

3 Put the flour on to a work surface and use your fist to make a hollow in the centre. Pour the eggs into the hollow. Add the sugar, ammonium carbonate or bicarbonate of soda, and salt. Mix together, then add the almonds.

4 Knead everything together thoroughly and shape the dough with your hands into several thick strips about 7.5cm/3in long, 6cm/2½in wide and 2.5cm/1in thick.

5 Slide the strips of dough on to the baking sheets and bake in the preheated oven for 10 minutes, or until golden.

6 Cut the strips into cookie-sized lengths, on the diagonal. Return them to the oven for a further 6 minutes, to crisp them.

7 Cool the cookies on a wire rack. Store in an airtight container for up to three months.

COOK'S TIP

The traditional raising agent is ammonium carbonate, but it is sometimes difficult to obtain. Bicarbonate of soda (baking soda) will also work, giving the cookies just enough of a lift during baking.

PER PORTION Energy 932kcal/3946kJ; Protein 19.7g; Carbohydrate 183.8g, of which sugars 107g; Fat 18.3g, of which saturates 2.5g; Cholesterol 152mg; Calcium 270mg; Fibre 4.8g; Sodium 68mg.

SOFT TUSCAN RICE CAKE
LA TORTA DI RISO

It is the rich, eggy and sticky quality of this cake that makes it the traditional Tuscan children's cake – despite containing a little brandy. Delicious and incredibly filling, it is like a home-made version of those little oval rice cakes you can buy at all Tuscan cafés and pâtisseries, called simply budino, which literally translates as 'pudding'. All Tuscans know that budino contains rice, but the name is always guaranteed to confuse anybody who does not come from the region. This is the classic version of the recipe, but you can vary the cake by adding nuts or candied fruits, if you like.

MAKES 1 CAKE

150g/5oz/⅔ cup short grain rice
1.2 litres/2 pints/5 cups milk
butter, for greasing
30ml/2 tbsp semolina
9 eggs
225g/8oz/generous 1 cup caster (superfine) sugar
45ml/3 tbsp brandy
grated rind of 1 unwaxed lemon

1 Put the rice and 750ml/1¼ pints/3 cups of the milk into a pan. Boil for 10 minutes, then drain, reserving the milk, which will have absorbed some of the starch from the rice. Set aside to cool slightly.

2 Preheat the oven to 180°C/350°F/Gas 4. Butter a 25cm/10in fixed-base cake tin (pan), thoroughly, and then sprinkle with the semolina. (Do not use a loose-based tin, or all the liquid will leak.) Turn the cake tin upside down and shake gently to remove any loose semolina.

3 Using an electric whisk, beat the eggs in a large bowl until foaming and pale yellow. Add the sugar gradually, beating constantly, then add the brandy and lemon rind. Stir well.

4 Add the rice and remaining milk (including the reserved milk). Pour into the cake tin.

5 Bake for 50 minutes, or until a cocktail stick (toothpick) inserted into the centre comes out clean. The cake should be well set and golden brown. Serve warm or cold.

COOK'S TIP

Don't worry about how runny the mixture seems when you pour it into the tin (pan); the finished cake should remain very moist and sticky when baked, and just be firm enough to slice neatly into portions.

PER CAKE Energy 2838kcal/11969kJ; Protein 111.3g; Carbohydrate 438.1g, of which sugars 295.1g; Fat 71.6g, of which saturates 25.9g; Cholesterol 1783mg; Calcium 1850mg; Fibre 0.6g; Sodium 1307mg.

TUSCAN CANDIED FRUIT-AND-NUT HARD CAKE
PANFORTE

Panforte is an old-fashioned sweetmeat, which dates back to the Renaissance and was reputedly first created in Siena. It is widely available in all good Italian food stores to buy ready made. Making it at home is a sticky but enjoyable process, and the end result, although a lot less perfect-looking than the ready-made version, tastes absolutely wonderful. You can normally buy the edible rice paper from good confectioners and many supermarkets, but otherwise simply line the baking tin with baking parchment and remove it before eating. Serve the panforte – a flat, shallow cake – sliced into thin strips. It is delicious with black coffee or dessert wine.

MAKES 1 CAKE

rice paper
200g/7oz/generous 1 cup unblanched almonds
225g/8oz/1 cup mixed (candied) peel, chopped
50g/2oz/¼ cup crystallized (candied) orange peel
130g/4½oz/generous ⅔ cup shelled walnuts
200g/7oz/1¾ cups plain (all-purpose) flour
5ml/1 tsp ground cinnamon
2.5ml/½ tsp ground allspice
2.5ml/½ tsp ground coriander
350g/12oz/1¾ cups caster (superfine) sugar
30ml/2 tbsp clear honey
15ml/1 tbsp each ground cinnamon and icing (confectioners') sugar, sifted together, for dusting

COOK'S TIP

A sugar thermometer is a good way to measure the temperature of the sugar accurately. However, you can always use the old-fashioned method: drop a tiny amount into a small cup of cold water. It is ready if it forms a perfect ball when you roll it between your thumb and index finger.

1 Preheat the oven to 150°C/300°F/Gas 2 and line a 25cm/10in a round shallow cake tin (pan) with rice paper or baking parchment.

2 Blanch 150g/5oz almonds by soaking them in hot water for about 1 minute, then removing the skins.

3 Lay the blanched almonds out on a baking sheet and toast them under a hot grill (broiler), turning occasionally, for about 5 minutes, or until golden. Chop them coarsely.

4 Put the chopped almonds into a food processor or blender with the chopped mixed peel, the crystallized orange peel and the walnuts. Whiz until it forms a rough mass. (Alternatively, chop very finely using a sharp knife.) Put the mixture on to a work surface.

5 Combine the nut and peel mixture with the remaining unblanched almonds and the flour and spices.

6 In a small pan, melt the sugar and honey together and boil until it reaches the 'soft ball stage' (119°C/238°F – see Cook's Tip).

7 Pour the hot sugar and honey mixture over the dry ingredients and mix well with a spatula and, when cooler, using your hands.

8 Press the mixture into the tin. Level in the tin using a spatula and bake in the oven for 30 minutes, or until golden.

9 Remove the cake from the oven and allow to cool on a wire rack.

10 Dust with the icing sugar and cinnamon mixture. Store it in an airtight container – it will keep for up to 1 year.

PER CAKE Energy 9564kcal/40476kJ; Protein 91g; Carbohydrate 1911.9g, of which sugars 1748g; Fat 225.7g, of which saturates 17.4g; Cholesterol 0mg; Calcium 4054mg; Fibre 134.8g; Sodium 6443mg.

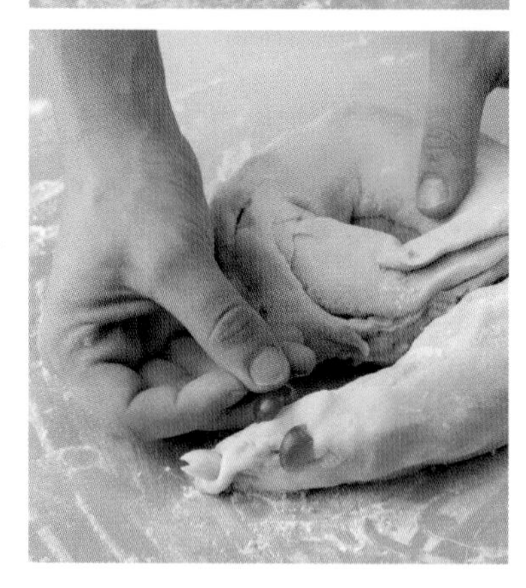

SNAKE-SHAPED CAKE
SERPENTONE

Apples and dried fruit, nuts and sugar are the main ingredients for this classic Umbrian cake. The pastry is quite unusual: made with olive oil, flour, sugar and water, it has quite a different texture to butter pastry. The decoration of the cake is where the cook's imagination takes flight – all kinds of expressions on the 'snake's' face can be created using a few carefully placed ingredients. Some local cooks add small coloured sweets (candies) to the snake, to represent scales. The cake is quite sweet, so should be served thinly sliced, with some chilled, fairly dry dessert wine.

1 Soak the sultanas in a bowl of warm water for about 20 minutes, until plump and softened.

2 Put the flour and caster sugar on to the work surface and add the oil and the salt. Add a little warm water, then knead gently to make a fairly solid pastry dough.

3 Cover the dough with a clean dish towel and leave to rest for about 20 minutes.

4 Preheat the oven to 180°C/350°F/Gas 4. Grease and flour a baking sheet.

5 Roll out the pastry on a floured surface as thinly as possible. Sprinkle the blanched, chopped almonds over the sheet of dough.

6 Drain the sultanas and pat them dry with kitchen paper. Spread them over the almonds, with the walnuts, apples, figs and prunes.

7 Sprinkle with the icing sugar and carefully roll the dough up on itself, to form a long cylinder. Twist the cylinder around to form a coiled snake shape and transfer on to the baking sheet.

8 To make the decoration, press the glacé cherries or coffee beans into place to represent the snake's eyes, and then press in the almond to represent the snake's tongue. Sprinkle with sugar.

9 Bake the cake for 40 minutes, or until golden. Cool on a wire rack before serving.

SERVES 6 TO 8

115g/4oz/⅔ cup sultanas (golden raisins)
225g/8oz/2 cups plain (all-purpose) flour, plus extra for dusting
115g/4oz/generous ½ cup caster (superfine) sugar
60ml/4 tbsp extra virgin olive oil, plus extra for greasing
pinch of salt
100–150ml/3½fl oz–¼ pint/scant ½ cup–⅔ cup warm water
50g/2oz/⅓ cup blanched almonds, coarsely chopped
8 walnuts, coarsely chopped
3 large eating apples, peeled and sliced
5 dried figs, chopped
5 ready-to-eat prunes, stoned (pitted) and chopped
30–45ml/2–3 tbsp icing (confectioners') sugar

FOR THE DECORATION

2 glacé (candied) cherries or 2 coffee beans
1 blanched almond
10–20ml/2–4 tsp caster (superfine) sugar

PER PORTION Energy 368kcal/1548kJ; Protein 5.8g; Carbohydrate 57.6g, of which sugars 36g; Fat 14.3g, of which saturates 1.5g; Cholesterol 0mg; Calcium 85mg; Fibre 2.6g; Sodium 8mg.

SPICED UMBRIAN CAKE
PANPEPATO

The Umbrian recipe for this Christmas speciality originates in the small town of Terni and its surrounding area. The Italian name literally translates as 'peppered bread', referring to the spices, which include some ground black pepper. The recipe has medieval roots and is typical of the kind of recipes attributed to that period of history, when spices and other expensive ingredients were used in generous quantities for special occasion dishes. Several versions of a similar recipe, with exactly the same name, exist in various parts of Central Italy.

MAKES 4 TO 6 CAKES

oil, for greasing
300g/11oz/scant 2 cups almonds
300g/11oz/scant 2 cups hazelnuts
1.5kg/3¼lb/8½ cups walnuts
300g/11oz/1½ cups honey
40–60ml/3–4 tbsp strongest possible espresso coffee
about 400ml/14fl oz/1⅔ cups boiled wine must (see Cook's Tip)
400g/14oz/scant 2 cups currants or sultanas (golden raisins), soaked in water for 20 minutes, or until plump and softened
300g/11oz/1⅓ cups crystallized (candied) citrus fruit, chopped
grated rind of 1 unwaxed orange
1.5ml/¼ tsp freshly grated nutmeg
1.5ml/¼ tsp ground black pepper
225g/8oz/2 cups pine nuts
700g/1lb 9oz dark (bittersweet) cooking chocolate, chopped
115g/4oz/1 cup unsweetened cocoa powder
200g/7oz/1 cup caster (superfine) sugar
about 200g/7oz/1¾ cups plain (all-purpose) flour
icing (confectioners') sugar, for dusting

COOK'S TIP

Boiled wine must is fermented grape juice, which has been reduced and sweetened by the process of boiling. If it proves hard to find, you can use a sweet red wine instead.

1 Preheat the oven to 180°C/350°F/Gas 4. Grease and flour a baking sheet.

2 Blanch the almonds by soaking them in hot water for about 1 minute, then removing the skins.

3 Lay the hazelnuts and the walnuts out on a baking sheet and toast them under a hot grill (broiler), turning occasionally, for about 5 minutes, or until golden.

4 Hold a few hazelnuts and walnuts at a time in a dish towel and rub off their skins. Repeat with all the remaining nuts. Chop them coarsely.

5 Put the honey into a pan and add the coffee and the wine must, stir together and warm gently.

6 Drain the currants or sultanas and pat dry with kitchen paper. Pile them on to a work surface.

7 Add the chopped crystallized citrus fruit, the grated orange rind, nutmeg and pepper, as well as the pine nuts, chocolate, cocoa powder and sugar.

8 Mix all these dry ingredients together with your hands, adding the warm honey mixture a little at a time. Gradually add the flour until you have achieved a manageable dough. (Add more flour or wine must as required.)

9 Shape this mixture into 4–6 small loaf shapes and lay them on the baking sheet. Bake them in the preheated oven for 10 minutes, or until golden.

10 Remove the cakes from the oven and allow to cool on a wire rack. Panpepato should be allowed to rest for 2–3 days after baking. To serve, dust with icing sugar and cut into slices.

PER CAKE Energy 2407kcal/10011kJ; Protein 44.3g; Carbohydrate 161.5g, of which sugars 138.7g; Fat 177.6g, of which saturates 25.6g; Cholesterol 6mg; Calcium 400mg; Fibre 14.1g; Sodium 248mg.

THE TRADITIONAL SWEET BREAD OF LUCCA
IL BUCCELLATO

The older, most elegant part of the city of Lucca, in north-western Tuscany, is surrounded by the old restored Renaissance city walls, so that it is possible to walk or cycle around the entire circumference and enjoy the view from the top of the wall. To make the experience even more pleasurable, each of the four principal sides is lined with a different kind of tree. This sweet bread, which is famously typical of this town, is presented annually for blessing as part of a special Mass in the city's cathedral.

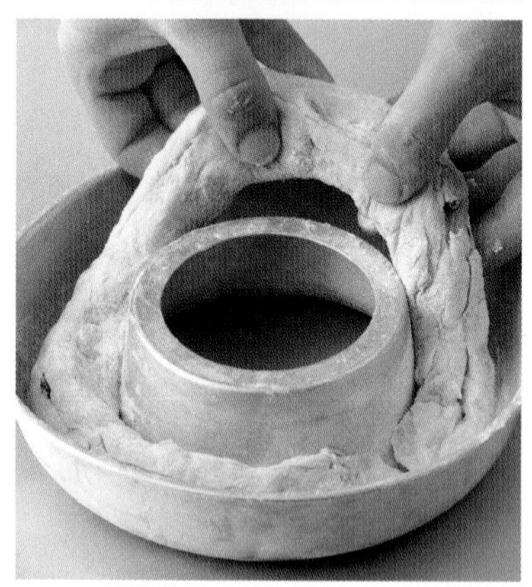

PER PORTION Energy 291kcal/1233kJ; Protein 5.9g; Carbohydrate 57.4g, of which sugars 23.1g; Fat 5.8g, of which saturates 3.1g; Cholesterol 50mg; Calcium 88mg; Fibre 1.7g; Sodium 80mg.

1 Put a handful of flour in a small bowl and crumble in the fresh yeast. Stirring constantly, trickle in enough tepid water to make a thick paste.

2 Cover the top of the bowl with clear film (plastic wrap) and place the bowl in a warm place for about 45 minutes, or until the flour has reacted with the yeast and the mixture has begun to expand.

3 Grease and flour a 20cm/8in ring mould. Preheat the oven to 150°C/300°F/Gas 2. Crush the fennel seeds to a powder in a spice grinder or using a mortar and pestle.

4 Put the remaining flour on to a work surface and use your fist to make a hollow in the centre.

5 Pour the sugar into the hollow, then add the melted butter, the beaten eggs, bicarbonate of soda, fennel seeds, mixed peel and sultanas, and grated lemon rind.

6 Put the yeasted flour starter into the hollow and roughly work all the ingredients together. Pour most of the remaining water into the hollow and begin to knead the ingredients together until you have an even, elastic dough, adding more water if required. Knead steadily for 10–15 minutes.

7 Roll out the dough into a cylinder, then turn it into a crown shape by joining the two ends together to form a circle.

8 Transfer the dough into the prepared ring mould. Mark the surface of the dough by cutting through it with a sharp knife all the way around the circle.

9 Leave to rise in a warm place, covered with oiled clear film, for about 1 hour or until doubled in size.

10 Lightly beat the egg white and brush it over the surface, then sprinkle with the icing sugar.

11 Bake the buccellato for 40 minutes, or until light golden in colour. Allow to cool slightly on a wire rack. Serve warm or cold.

SERVES 10

- 450g/1lb/4 cups plain (all-purpose) flour
- 20g/¾oz fresh yeast
- about 250ml/8fl oz/1 cup tepid water
- 15ml/1 tbsp fennel seeds
- 175g/6oz caster (superfine) sugar
- 50g/2oz/¼ cup unsalted butter, melted
- 2 eggs, beaten
- 5ml/1 tsp bicarbonate of soda (baking soda)
- 70g/2¾oz/½ cup mixed (candied) peel and sultanas (golden raisins)
- grated rind of ½ unwaxed lemon
- oil, for greasing
- flour, for dusting
- 1 egg white
- icing (confectioners') sugar, for dusting

CARNIVAL FRITTERS
SFRAPPÉ

During Carnival, people all over Italy have always celebrated out on the streets, especially on Shrove Tuesday and the Thursday after Ash Wednesday, or Giovedi Grasso in Italian. This is the last important opportunity for a lot of noise and fun before the rigours of Lent really set in. Many types of street food, or at least food that was once cooked on the streets, are attached in some way to this period, most of them sweet and deep-fried in oil according to tradition. This particular recipe is from Le Marche, but sfrappé are made in various ways all over Italy. They are as much a part of the Carnival spirit in Italy as the masks and costumes, the endless practical jokes and street parading that happens in towns and cities all over the country.

1 In a large bowl, mix together the flour, butter, lard or white cooking fat, egg yolks and whole egg, sugar, salt, lemon juice and Mistra, if using.

2 Gently knead to make a soft ball of dough, not dissimilar to fresh pasta dough. If dry, add a little dry white wine. Leave the dough to rest, covered with a clean dish towel, for about 30 minutes.

3 Put the dough on a lightly floured surface and roll it out thinly, then cut it into long, wide ribbons, using a pastry wheel or sharp knife.

4 Heat the oil in a large pan until a small cube of bread dropped into it sizzles instantly. Carefully drop a few sfrappé into the oil, about six or seven in every batch.

5 As soon as they become golden and puffed up and are floating on the surface of the oil, scoop them out with a slotted spoon and drain thoroughly on kitchen paper.

6 Dust the fritters with icing sugar, sprinkle with Alchermes, if using, and serve warm with chilled dessert wine.

SERVES 8

- 450g/1lb/4 cups plain (all-purpose) flour, plus extra for dusting
- 50g/2oz/¼ cup unsalted butter, lard or white cooking fat
- 2 egg yolks
- 1 egg
- 15ml/1 tbsp caster (superfine) sugar
- pinch of salt
- a few drops of lemon juice
- 30ml/2 tbsp Mistra liqueur (optional)
- dry white wine, if needed
- sunflower oil, for deep-frying
- icing (confectioners') sugar, for dusting
- Alchermes liqueur, for sprinkling (optional)
- chilled dessert wine, to serve

COOK'S TIP

You can omit the Mistra and Alchermes liqueurs if you are planning to serve these fritters to children.

PER PORTION Energy 359kcal/1506kJ; Protein 6.1g; Carbohydrate 45.7g, of which sugars 2.8g; Fat 18.2g, of which saturates 5.2g; Cholesterol 65mg; Calcium 87mg; Fibre 1.7g; Sodium 51mg.

MAKES 6

extra virgin olive oil, for greasing and drizzling
semolina or polenta flour, for dusting
450g/1lb Basic Bread Dough
plain (all-purpose) flour, for dusting
450g/1lb fresh black or white grapes, seedless
15–30ml/1–2 tbsp caster (superfine) sugar

TUSCAN GRAPE-HARVEST FOCACCIA
SCHIACCIATA D'UVA

This type of sweet bread is made around the time of the wine harvest – vendemmia – when there is a bountiful supply of fresh, sweet grapes around. You need to squash the grapes down well into the top of the focaccia base, using plenty of sugar to bring out the flavour of the fruit. The amount of sugar you need will depend on the sweetness of the grapes. The end result looks beautiful and tastes delicious. During the vendemmia, all the smartest cafés in Florence and the surrounding areas will be selling slices of this traditional focaccia to celebrate the arrival of the new wine.

1 Preheat the oven to 220°C/425°F/Gas 7. Oil two baking sheets generously and dust with semolina or polenta flour.

2 Divide the dough into six portions. On a floured work surface, roll them in to 1cm/½ in thick circles and place on the baking sheets.

3 Drizzle the surface of each schiacciata with a little oil, then cover each one with grapes.

4 Press the grapes down into the dough with the flat of your hand. Sprinkle with the sugar and bake for 15–20 minutes, or until cooked through. Serve warm or cold.

PER PORTION Energy 337kcal/1432kJ; Protein 7.4g; Carbohydrate 75.1g, of which sugars 17.9g; Fat 2.9g, of which saturates 0.3g; Cholesterol 0mg; Calcium 117mg; Fibre 2.9g; Sodium 4mg.

INDEX

AUTHOR'S ACKNOWLEDGEMENTS
This book is dedicated to the memory of my courageous and eternally stylish friend Helen Trent.

PUBLISHER'S ACKNOWLEDGEMENTS
The publishers would like to thank the following for permission to reproduce their images (t = top, b = bottom, l = left and r = right): p7tl Gillian Price/Alamy; p7tr mediacolor's/Alamy; p7b funkyfood London – Paul Williams/Alamy; p8bl Wedding banquet of Grand Duke Ferdinand I of Tuscany (1549-1600), 1590 by Passignano, Domenico Cresti (c.1560-1636) Kunsthistorisches Museum, Vienna, Austria/The Bridgeman Art Library; p8br Jon Arnold Images Ltd/ Alamy; p9tl Owen Franken/Corbis; p9tr iStockphoto; p10b Atlantide Phototravel/Corbis; p11tl John Warburton-Lee Photography/Alamy; p11tr iStockphoto; p12tl Image France/ Alamy; p12tr Sandra Raccanello/ Grand Tour/Corbis; p13tr Maurice Joseph/Alamy; p13bl iStockphoto; p14tr Giuseppe Benaglio/Alamy; p14bl The Photolibrary Wales/Alamy; p15tl Christine Webb/Alamy; p15tr Caro/Alamy; p32r, p35l, p38r, p48r, p84r, p92r, p95l, p118r, p108r, p113l, p122r iStockphoto.